Beyond My Adobe Schoolhouse

NASARIO GARCÍA

Beyond
My Life
My Adobe
in Education
Schoolhouse

University of New Mexico Press   Albuquerque

ISBN 978-0-8263-6700-6 (paper)
ISBN 978-0-8263-6701-3 (ePub)

Library of Congress Control Number: 2024941380

Founded in 1889, the University of New Mexico sits on the traditional homelands of the Pueblo of Sandia. The original peoples of New Mexico—Pueblo, Navajo, and Apache—since time immemorial have deep connections to the land and have made significant contributions to the broader community statewide. We honor the land itself and those who remain stewards of this land throughout the generations and also acknowledge our committed relationship to Indigenous peoples. We gratefully recognize our history.

Cover images adapted from images courtesy of Nasario García

Frontispiece: Nasario García, University of Southern Colorado, 1985.

Designed by Isaac Morris

Composed in Bookmania, Covik Sans and Times New Roman

To
my dear wife,
whose support
in graduate school
and throughout my
academic career
never waned.

Janice M. Smith-García, November 21,
1964, Granada, Spain.

Never wear your PhD on your sleeve.
You'll only belittle and embarrass yourself.

—ALBERT R. LOPES, PHD

The best way to end a bad beginning . . .
is to begin a good ending.

—ZIGGY AND FRIENDS, INC.

CONTENTS

ACKNOWLEDGMENTS

No work regardless of its magnitude can see the light of day without the expertise of individuals such as those I've had the privilege of working with at UNM Press. At the forefront there is Elise McHugh, senior acquisition editor, whose constant encouragement of my work over the years has been unabated. A special thanks goes to James Ayers, editorial, design, and production manager, for his overarching support; Isaac Morris, the designer of the elegant book cover; and Min Marcus, who prepared all the materials. A note of gratitude is also hereby expressed to Anna Pohlod, editor, and Bridget Manzella, copyeditor, both of whom oversaw the final version of my book. And a salute goes to Don Redpath, sales and marketing manager, for publicizing my work. Last but not least, I wish to extend my heartfelt thanks to Stephen Hull, director, for his overall help.

INTRODUCTION

Beyond My Adobe Schoolhouse: My Life in Education is not an exercise in self-glorification and adulation. Rather, my memoir takes the reader on an extraordinary journey that recounts the educational experiences I enjoyed and the challenges I encountered in public schools and higher education. Secondly, my autobiography is a tribute to those individuals who on the one hand motivated me to seek an education while others steered me toward a long-standing career in academia.

My remembrances may not offer anything startling or novel in terms of accomplishments, but I trust that they are at least a keen reminder of personal hard work, sacrifices, and good fortune. I started first grade in 1943 at La Mesa School at Rincón del Cochino in the Río Puerco Valley southeast of Chaco Canyon (see map) in a one-room adobe schoolhouse. My two years at La Mesa were followed by ten years (1945–1955) in the Albuquerque Public School system.

After serving two years in the military (1955–1957), I began my studies at the University of New Mexico. There I earned a BA in Spanish (1962) and an MA in Portuguese (1963).

In 1966, following a year of doctoral courses (*cursos monográficos*) at the University of Granada, Spain, I enrolled in the Department of Romance Languages and Literatures at the University of Pittsburgh. I was awarded a PhD in 1972. To go from a one-room schoolhouse grades one through eight and ultimately attend classes at the forty-two-story Cathedral of Learning—the tallest educational building in the United States—exceeded my wildest dreams.

But I did not reach those proud heights, literally and metaphorically, alone. Foremost supporters of my educational voyage were my delightful parents for whom a formal education was never within their grasp. My father, the youngest of six siblings in the Río Puerco Valley where he was born and raised, rode a horse to school in the 1910s, but he dropped out of school in the fifth grade to help his parents with ranch/farm chores. In contrast, my mother, born in the San Miguel Mountains near Cuba, New Mexico, never attended a day of school.

When I was a small boy Dad worked for the Works Progress Administration (WPA) and Civilian Conservation Corps (CCC) camps in the Río Puerco Valley to support his young family at the height of the Great Depression. The back-breaking jobs left an indelible impression on him vis-à-vis the importance of education.

Mom's appreciation for education on the other hand stemmed more from intuition and the hard work of maintaining a household and raising eight children. She knew once I started as a freshman at the University of New Mexico that I was on financial straits. Hence, she'd wash and iron my clothes. I made my weekly treks to visit her and to pick up my clothing at Los Ranchos de Alburquerque where my family settled. "Ahi tienes, hijito, pa que estés bien pantera en la universidá." (There you are, my dear son, so that you look dapper at the university.) Her inspiring and reassuring words still ring clear and distinctly.

Besides my father and mother, a core of professors at the University of New Mexico encouraged me to major in languages, a fortuitous suggestion as it turned out. The names of Albert R. Lopes, Francis M. Kercheville, and Ramón J. Sender remain indelibly etched in my mind. I am indebted to each one for their inspiration and good counsel, above all Dr. Lopes, the consummate master teacher who remained a constant motivator. He persuaded me to pursue a career in academia despite my doubts about reaching for the lofty goal of becoming a university professor.

Most of my professors at the graduate and undergraduate level were good to excellent teachers. At the same time, I had my share of dull, ill-prepared, and uninspiring instructors who by all indications either chose the wrong profession or were ill-suited for teaching. Others were intellectually pompous and condescending.

From the onset of my teaching career I vowed to pattern myself after the good teachers as well as not to replicate those pedagogical shortcomings of mediocre or egotistical professors. I believed, too, as I matured in the classroom, that to excel as a teacher it behooved you to be well-prepared at all times. Being honest with your students if you didn't know the answer to a question was likewise of utmost importance.

My professional life lured me away from New Mexico for more than twenty years. This enabled me to view academia from a cosmopolitan perspective rather than simply a regional or a local one. I started my teaching career in 1965 at Chatham College, an outstanding girls' liberal arts institution in Pittsburgh. That set me on a path of thirty-six years of extraordinary and unforgettable pedagogical experiences that included Illinois, Colorado, and ultimately New Mexico.

Regardless of the state or university, overall my tenure at each one by and large proved enriching. The students in Pittsburgh who hailed primarily from affluent families were eminently well prepared for college work. The antithesis was often the case with students from blue-collar enclaves such as Cicero, a suburb of Chicago, whom I taught at Northern Illinois University. On returning to Colorado and

New Mexico, countless Hispanic students in my classes were raised in rural communities. As a consequence they arrived on campus with linguistic problems similar to those that bedeviled me as a university freshman. I could relate to their predicament since I too spent the formative years of my youth in the hinterland as well with virtually no exposure to the rudiments of the English language.

As a professor, staying active in professional and scholarly activities was fundamental. I sincerely believe that these undertakings enriched me, and by extension, my students. To meet professors and students from Spain (some of whom I have remained friends with) as a guest lecturer at the *Curso de Verano* sponsored by the Universidad Complutense de Madrid was special. Being a presenter at the historic University of Alcalá de Henares too was special. At both institutions I had the distinct honor of sharing information connecting the richness of Spanish and my own culture of northern New Mexico to Spain.

But a capstone to these cultural exchanges transpired at the Casa América in Madrid when the Príncipe Felipe de Asturias, now the King of Spain, met privately with a group of us New Mexicans.

Besides Spain, I was invited to lecture at language conferences in Portugal, Mexico, Guatemala, Costa Rica, Puerto Rico, Canada, and of course across the United States. (During my academic career I visited twenty-four European and Latin American countries including China (see Appendix A).) In addition to sharing the long-standing Hispano language and culture of New Mexico (e.g., folklore and oral history), I addressed various facets of Chicano literature in the American Southwest in general and New Mexico in particular.

A reciprocal exchange of cross-cultural points of view with colleagues and students abroad and in this country was edifying. I believe that this type of give-and-take made me a better teacher and trustfully a more compassionate human being.

Throughout my academic career I enjoyed a multitude of joyful moments that I treasure to this day. My tenure at Chatham College (1965–1969) in Pittsburgh stands out. The professional attitude of administrators coupled with the intellectual enthusiasm and curiosity among faculty and students was inspirational and gratifying.

My years (1973–1986) at the University of Southern Colorado (USC) in Pueblo likewise are memorable indeed and second to none. Numerous times I was honored with the Owl Awards by the academic administration, the language department, and/or students for my teaching and scholarship. But aside from the foregoing awards the president and academic vice president never failed to send letters of commendation pursuant to my community service at large.

A highpoint ancillary to my duties and responsibilities at the University of Southern Colorado transpired in 1979. The Colorado Commission on Libraries selected me as a delegate-at-large to the White House Conference on Libraries and Information Services in Washington, DC. Jimmy Carter was president at that time. As a conferee I had the distinct honor of being invited by members of Congress to testify before a United States Senate and House Education Committee on illiteracy among Hispanics in the United States.

Other professional engagements transpired toward the end of my long-standing career. In 1990–1991, I was elected vice president/president, one before the other, of the American Association of Teachers of Spanish and Portuguese (AATSP). This was truly a prestigious honor for I was only the second native New Mexican to hold that position since the founding of the organization in 1917. My election coincided with a return to the classroom in 1991 after I served five memorable—and not so memorable—years (1986–1991) as dean of the School of Liberal and Fine Arts at New Mexico Highlands University. I retired from academia in 2001.

All through my thirty-six years in higher education I did my best to represent my profession with integrity. I devoted endless energy toward all three facets of my career: teaching, scholarship, and community service. Whatever recognition I garnered or was accorded in these areas, I am beholden to appreciative administrators and colleagues, but above all else I am indebted to my loyal and erstwhile students.

Not to be forgotten are those stars and stalwarts who helped me carve out a niche in academia. Their benevolent voices and those of my beloved parents resonate in one fashion or another across the pages of *Beyond My Adobe Schoolhouse: My Life in Education.*

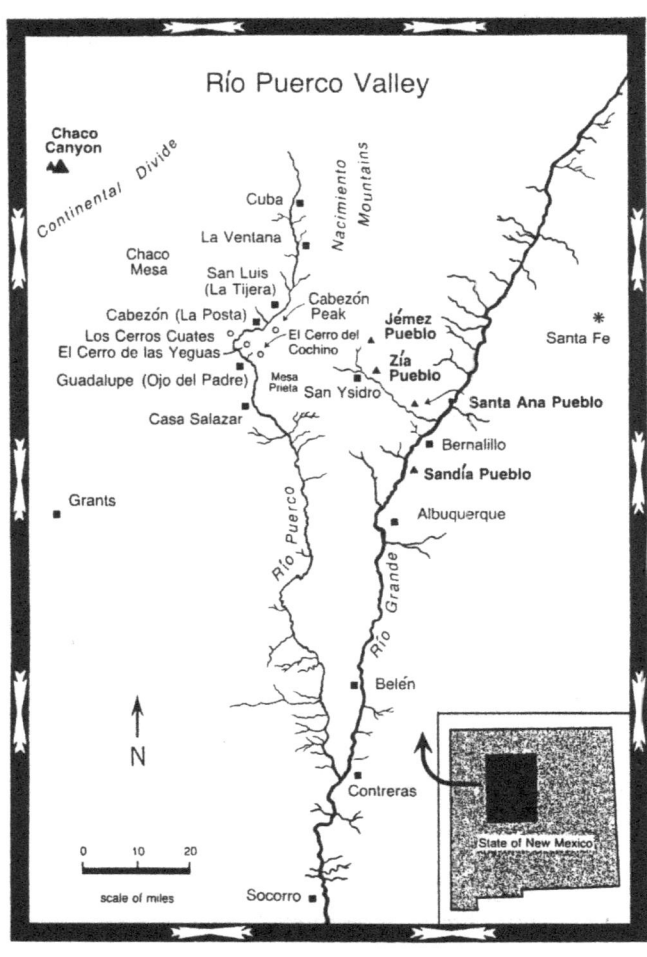

The Beginning

Long Ago

LOOKING ACROSS TIME AND SPACE, I never envisioned that once I started first grade in a one-room adobe schoolhouse I would spend the rest of my life in the classroom (except two years in the military). To seek a formal education, earn several degrees, including a PhD, and to become a university professor of Hispanic languages and literatures (on occasion I taught Portuguese) at various universities across the United States, speaks broadly to my educational experience. Plus I had the good fortune to lecture in countries like Spain, Canada, Puerto Rico, Mexico, Peru, and Costa Rica.

For a kid like me who spent the formative years of his life in rural New Mexico* during the late 1930s and early 1940s, pipe dreams such as becoming an academic were rare. This was especially true in rural schools like mine where an eighth-grade education was the highest level offered by the state's school system. Though education was tacitly mentioned at home, helping one's parents carve out an existence from the land and raising domestic animals for family consumption took precedence over schooling.

My educational career began 1943 in a remote part of New Mexico called the Río Puerco Valley approximately fifty miles southeast

---

* For a comprehensive look at my childhood in the Río Puerco Valley, I suggest *Hoe, Heaven, and Hell: My Boyhood in Rural New Mexico* (2015). Visit my website, https://nasariogarcia.com, for additional information and awards.

of the renowned Chaco Canyon. Mom, Dad, my siblings, and I lived on my paternal grandparents' ranch in a two-room adobe house that I called my *casita*. Our village, Ojo del Padre (Guadalupe in more modern times), was a scant two miles west of our home across the Río Puerco. The famous Cabezón Peak, a majestic volcanic plug, loomed to the north whereas the Río Puerco ran about three hundred feet south of our house. La Mesa Prieta, the Black Mesa, also a landmark of note, rested to the east near La Mesa School where I started first grade.

One Friday afternoon on his way home from his government job building roads, fences, and *represas*, small pools of water for animals, Dad stopped at don Ricardo Heller's General Store at the historic village of Cabezón located a few miles north of our house. There he bought me a Big Chief Tablet, a pencil, and a box of crayons, or Crayolas, a word that sounded more like Spanish than English. Although nothing flamboyant, these three self-effacing school items were the bare necessities for a first grader beginning his education.

The most important topic at suppertime on Sunday was not farm or household chores but rather my first day of school come Monday morning in early September. I was the eldest child—seven more siblings came later—and therefore the first offspring to attend school. Mom was jubilant. And Dad was happy, too, but more reserved in showing emotions; that was his nature. "¿Quieres que le haga punta a tu lápiz?" (Do you want me to sharpen your pencil?) Dad asked while we ate our dessert and he reached for his pocketknife in the leather holder attached to his belt. "No, apá," I responded. "Cousin Juan says they have a little machine [*maquinita*] at school for sharpening pencils. I'll wait till I get to school tomorrow."

Bedtime came, and Mom tucked me into bed and blessed me. The restless night from the excitement as well as jitteriness of starting school seemed long in comparison to other nights. Before I knew it, Mom came to shake me out of bed. "¡Anda! ¡Levántate! Se te

School bus that Nasario García rode to school.

van a pegar las sábanas" (Come! Up, up! The bedsheets are going to stick to you), she said with a wry but happy smile.

After I ate my oatmeal, a warm flour tortilla, and drank a glass of fresh milk, I put on my brand-new bib overalls, high top shoes (I called them *matavíboras*, or snake killers), and my white shirt. I proceeded to neatly tuck my school belongings in a flour bag; it would serve as my knapsack (*mochila*). Inside I also put my brown paper sack with my lunch, water, and a cloth napkin. I was prepared for the day's adventure that awaited me.

Before long the crucial moment of having to catch my uncle Antonio's school bus had arrived. I sat at the kitchen table and watched Mom's Westclox tick away before she and I headed for the "bus stop" about seventy feet from our house. My uncle was known for being prompt. He also tended to be a bit cantankerous, thus Mom made sure I was there by eight o'clock or else he'd probably get mad if he had to wait for me.

All of a sudden I heard the motor roaring. The dust flew as he rounded the butte next to our house. He stopped momentarily by his home down the hill to pick up my cousins Galo, Juan, and Julia who was my age.

Mom hugged me and offered her blessings, something she did whenever I left home on a trip, but today's journey, unlike others, was special. It was, after all, my first day of school.

Uncle Antonio stopped, got out of the yellow school bus, and opened the rear doors. I hopped in. I knew my cousins, of course, as well as Alonso and Emilia Gonzales whose mother was my catechism teacher and a well-respected *rezadora* (prayer leader) in our village, but the Jaramillo kids from Santa Clara were relative strangers. Four or five of us sat snuggly on either side of the bus facing each other (no seat belts) in the small bus that, on reflection, seemed large to me. Except for Dad's *carrito* (old clunker) as he called it, I had never ridden in another vehicle.

The trip to La Mesa School from my house under perfect weather conditions took about fifteen to twenty minutes amid some bouncing. The winding dirt road traversed the Cañada del Camino, a ravine populated with prairie dogs. The Cerro Chivato loomed in the background. One or two picturesque buttes dotted the landscape adjacent to the Montaños' household where we stopped to pick up Loyola whom I knew because his parents and mine were good friends. By the time we got to school, I guesstimated that it was 8:15 or so (no pupils wore a watch) with ample time left before school started at 8:30.

My uncle got down and swung open the rear doors. One by one we jumped off the bus. Everyone scattered about on the playground and joined the Valencia kids who lived practically next door where the teacher boarded. The Armijo kids who lived not far south of the school were already there as well. They usually came on horseback since Mr. Jorge Valencia had a corral where he fed the horses and gave them water throughout the day.

Some of my schoolmates hadn't seen each other throughout the summer; they were happy to renew acquaintances. The hollering and cheering could be heard bouncing off the sandstone boulders adjacent to La Mesa School. Excitement was in the air!

My cousin Juan was going to be in the second grade. Aware that I was new to the school he invited me inside the one-room school-house. "Aquí tienes tu casa" (Here's your home), he said to me. "This is where we'll be spending the next nine months," he uttered in Spanish.

The school building was rectangular in shape with two windows on either side. Toward the back as you entered there was a small desk for the teacher with a blackboard hanging on the wall. To one side of the desk was a five-gallon wooden barrel wrapped in burlap filled with drinking water for the students. Hanging from a nail attached to the barrel was an aluminum dipper and a dish towel to wipe it clean after one took a sip or two of water. Mr. Valencia supplied the water. In the middle of the room was a wood-burning pot belly stove. He also provided the wood, but it was the older boys' responsibility to stoke it and keep the fire going in the winter months. Now being the fall season that was not a chore they had to contend with.

"Buenos días, good morning, Juan. What a pleasure to see you! Who is this with you?"

"Miss Montoya," Juan responded in Spanish since I didn't know any English, "This is my cousin. He's new this year."

"¡Bienvenido! Welcome to La Mesa School! I think you'll like it here," Miss Montoya said. "¿Cómo te llamas?" (What is your name?).

"Yo me llamo Nasario, pero en casa me llaman Junie." (My name is Nasario, but at home they call me Junie.)

A few minutes later Miss Montoya rang a handbell to catch everyone's attention. "Okay. I want everyone to line up in front of the school."

The students headed by the older ones who by now knew the

routine didn't dillydally. They formed two columns and led the way inside the one-room schoolhouse. Everyone scurried for an empty desk that seated two students. As was predictable, those who knew each other or were friends sat together. Juan and I sat at one desk. Once everyone was seated, Miss Montoya stood in front of the class. Silence ensued. You could sense that she commanded respect from her students.

"¡Bienvenidos a todos! Welcome everybody! It gives me great pleasure (me da mucho gusto) to greet those students who are new this year." Her partial greetings in Spanish were for the benefit of first-grade pupils like me who knew no English whatsoever.

In her left hand, Miss Montoya had a white piece of paper with the students' names. She read them aloud: first graders first, second graders next, and so forth, until she got to the eighth-grade students. As each student raised his or her right hand, Miss Montoya proceeded to make desk assignments, randomly mixing first graders with fifth graders and the like. This ensured breaking up the so-called "buddy system," especially among the lower grades. Learning, as I found out later, was uppermost in Miss Montoya's mind since eighth graders would be tutoring students in the lower grades. These grades comprised the largest number of students and for that reason needed more help reading, solving math problems and so on as the school year progressed.

Miss Montoya switched between Spanish and English, indeed a foreign language for all of us. Using Spanish eased the transition from home to school for beginners like me, but learning English still turned out to be a formidable undertaking. The tendency to invoke Spanish in the classroom was much easier than to use English. That was certainly true on the school grounds when students were free to mingle.

A drawback for the older students—as well as the teacher— was the fact that most of them had not practiced their English skills throughout the summer. Learning English was akin to running in place or taking one step forward and two steps backward.

Notwithstanding drawbacks, Miss Montoya somehow moved things along. For the moment, whatever she had just said, more than half the students raised their pencils in the air at which point I impulsively held my unsharpened pencil above my head and said, ¿Puedo hacerle punta a mi lápiz?" (May I sharpen my pencil?) These were the first words I ever uttered in school—and no one snickered or made faces at me. "Desde hoy en adelante vamos hablar inglés en la clase" (From this day forward we're going to speak English in class), Miss Montoya cautioned tactfully. Her words, I learned in the days, weeks, and months ahead, were the trademark of a conscientious and sensitive teacher. Somehow she was adept at balancing the use of English and Spanish with utmost discretion. Scolding us for using Spanish in class was not her nature.

Before I knew it, Miss Montoya rang the bell. According to the clock on her desk it was 10:30 and time for the morning's fifteen-minute recess. This extracurricular activity was a novelty to me and the rest of the first graders. The playground instantaneously turned into a flurry of activity. Some kids hollered or screamed in screeching voices as they rode the swings or seesaws. The young students were more docile: the boys shot marbles and the girls played hopscotch or jumped rope. The older boys and one or two girls batted softballs or played catch. Recess was also an opportunity to use the communal *escusao*, or outhouse. (Indoor plumbing in the countryside was unheard of.)

After recess Miss Montoya spent the rest of the morning explaining what a typical day would be like in the classroom. For example, the older students once they had finished their class assignments were to help and tutor the younger ones in reading, writing or solving math problems. That is why fifth, sixth, seventh, and eighth graders were seated at desks with the lower grades. This approach to learning was a practical way of maximizing class time for Miss Montoya who could not teach all grades at once.

Before long, it was lunchtime. We had approximately one hour—from twelve to one o'clock. If the weather was good we either ate our lunch in the schoolhouse or outdoors, but the Valencia kids went home to eat. As for Miss Montoya, she ate her lunch at her desk, but later as the school year progressed she joined the Valencia family for the noon meal as part of her room and board. In her absence one or two eighth graders were left in charge at lunchtime.

Since it was my first day of school, Cousin Juan and I lunched together. The fall weather was pleasant, consequently, we propped ourselves up against an outside wall that provided a bit of shade at high noon. Inside my white flour sack was the brown paper bag with my lunch of scrambled egg and potatoes wrapped in a flour tortilla, the forerunner of today's ubiquitous so-called burrito that Mom prepared for me. A *mantelito*, cloth napkin, and a small Mason jar of water were in the flour bag as well. For dessert, Mom had packed two *bizcochitos* (cinnamon anise cookies). I said my blessing and thought of Mom who always insisted that we children say grace. "Gracias a Dios que nos da el pan de cada día. Amén." (Thanks be to God who gives us our daily bread. Amen.) These were common words at home before lunch and dinnertime, though breakfast for some unexplained reason was exempt.

Following lunch, Juan and I joined other kids our age on the playground. Mingling with strangers, except for Loyola Montaño whom I knew, was a new experience. We horsed around, and I quickly became accustomed to the surroundings and my new playmates. Before long, the lunch hour had flown by. Once again we heard the ting-a-ling coming from Miss Montoya's goat bell that Mr. Valencia loaned her. He and his wife Melecia were known for raising lots of goats and making goat cheese.

We formed two columns in front of the schoolhouse, a scene

that would be replicated time and again throughout the year unless there was inclement weather. For now the younger kids lined up first, and the older students were last. Hereafter, this was to be the order of lining up and filing into the schoolhouse before assuming our designated seats. The entire sequence was done in an orderly fashion and characteristic of the discipline and respect that Miss Montoya commanded—and expected—from her students. She was, after all, the *maestra*, teacher and master of her craft who like most teachers in rural communities personified respect and stood for a paragon of knowledge.

As soon as everyone was seated, Miss Montoya spoke again mixing English and Spanish to make sure everyone understood her. "Bueno, atención por favor." (Okay, please let me have your attention.) "As the older students know, I take teaching very seriously so, as a reminder to them as well as for the benefit of the new students, I want to share with you a few rules of behavior in the classroom. These are things you are not—I emphasize, not—to do to disrupt the class."

Here in random order are those don'ts that Miss Montoya recited in English and explained in Spanish that I can still recall to this day:

> You will NOT talk out of turn unless you're asked to by the teacher.
> You will NOT chew and crack gum.
> You will NOT bother your classmate in front or behind you.
> You will NOT shoot spit wads at your classmates.
> You will NOT build or fly paper airplanes.

The majority of the forgoing warnings were not all unambiguous to me or the new students, but I learned in due time that most of the rules were aimed at the older boys with a penchant for cutting up in class. As to punishment, it varied according to the infraction. For instance, a student could be made to stand in a corner of the classroom facing the wall; or, he had to kneel on the floor with pant legs rolled up to the knees with hands folded in front while the students, the girls in particular, gawked at him. If a boy was caught chewing and cracking gum in a girl's ear, he had to apologize to her in front of the entire class or stand in front of the class with the gum stuck to his forehead. Regardless of the punishment, it was not only demeaning but also humiliating to the culprit's ego. Repeat offenders, I learned later on, were rare.

No sooner had Miss Montoya read her list of warnings than the afternoon recess had arrived. The outdoor activities were no different from the morning's break.

After we lined up and entered the classroom, Miss Montoya had everyone rest their heads on top of the desk for about three to five minutes. Murmuring of sorts was barely audible among some students as the teacher walked up and down the classroom. She was mostly concerned about the younger kids getting some rest.

"Bueno. Everyone sit up straight, take a deep breath, and listen carefully," Miss Montoya said. "All of you will be assigned a book for the school year depending on whether you're a first grader, second grader, and so on. Each one of you is responsible for taking care of your personal book so please remember the following words," which she wrote on the blackboard both in Spanish and English:

Si yo este libro me perdiera,	If I should lose this book,
como puede suceder,	as it's bound to happen,
le pido al que lo hallara,	I ask whoever finds it,
que me lo sepa devolver.	to have the decency to return it me.
Y si fuera de uñas largas,	And should he have sticky fingers,
y con poco entendimiento,	and is a bit unprincipled,
le pido que se acuerde	I ask him to remember
del séptimo mandamiento.	the seventh commandment.*

---

* Thou shall not steal.

From this moment forward, the stage was set for the teaching-learning drama that was to unfold in the coming weeks and months. Each grade level individually and collectively posed a variety of pedagogical challenges not only for Miss Montoya but for us students as well.

Her clock rang at precisely three o'clock. She bid us goodbye as my first day of school came to an end. I looked out the window next to my desk and saw my uncle Antonio waiting with the back doors to his school bus propped open. I walked at a fast pace anxious to hop in and even more eager to get home to share the day's experiences with Mom.

My cousins and the rest of us bounced and jostled each other as my uncle navigated the winding sandy road. He appeared to be going really fast, but that was the sensation on dirt roads if the hard surface felt like a washboard. It was frightening. I learned that feeling from riding in Dad's old Chevrolet car. I looked out the bus's small rearview windows and all I could see was a trail of dust. After an abrupt stop that covered the bus with powdery dust, Loyola jumped off the bus. From his house to mine was a mere seven to ten minutes before my uncle came to another screeching halt, but this time there was no dust since the road next to my house was hard and dry as an adobe brick.

I barely waited for Uncle Antonio to open the rear doors. As he pried them open I jumped and hit the ground hard with my flour sack and contents tightly gripped in my right hand, I sprinted the short distance to my casita. I dashed in the kitchen itching to see Mom and to share my first day's school experience with her.

"¡Hijito!¡Qué remolino ni que nada!" (What a whirlwind!), she said. "And how was school? Come, tell me all about it . . . and don't forget to change into your playing clothes."

"Bueno, amá, but first I have to get me something to eat. I'm a little hungry."

I grabbed a cold flour tortilla that was wrapped in a dish towel, slapped a thin layer of lard, and sprinkled a dash of salt on it. I took my first bite.

Afterward I described to Mom my first day of schooling at La Mesa School near El Rincón del Cochino. This was a canyon-like area named in honor of a man who purportedly raised a multitude of hogs for a living. Mom, who never attended a day of school in her life, listened attentively while I related verbatim the day's activities. She had a twinkle in her eyes. As for me, I was exhausted by the time I finished.

Time elapsed, as it must, but day by day I learned something new at school, both in the classroom as well as out on the play area. Not everything was pleasant, however. For example, I dislocated my right elbow after the older boys chased me to de-pant me in front of the girls. I ran to elude them, climbed a wooden gate to Mr. Valencia's horse corral, and jumped. When I landed, I hit my elbow on a rock. The pain was unbearable. This episode remains embedded in my psyche to this day. My cousin Galo acted as the rogue of the group. De-panting was a game he and the Jaramillo brothers, Cándido and Feliz, played. The victims invariably were first graders like me.

But boys must be boys, and the girls were not exempt from their antics. They were a prime target in the classroom regardless of Miss Montoya's list of "don'ts." On more than one occasion a boy pelted a girl on the butt but with *tetones*, green pods from a nearby cotton-wood tree. The teacher had a knack for guessing who the culprit was, or she could determine by the look on his face. Punishment, which could be humiliating to the troublemaker, was meted out without hesitation. Potential scalawags took heed and oftentimes learned not to engage in such tomfooleries unless they were prepared to bear the consequences.

As the fall term progressed, a bright light of learning descended on me. Of the three skills—reading, writing, and speaking—I found reading to be the most alluring. Still, writing, even in cryptic phrases, posed extreme challenges for me and most of the other students regardless of grade level. Speaking was a tad easier since it somehow paralleled reading in terms of the enunciation of words. But reading either silently or aloud was not without its drawbacks due to the inference of Spanish. The *v*'s turned into *b*'s (very > bery). The letter *s* resulted in *es* (school > eschool), and the initial English *r* became *rr* as in Spanish (run > rrun). Most of us thought intuitively that by altering the pronunciation of certain consonants in English they would somehow sound better when in fact it made matters worse (e.g., *ch* became *sh* as in church > shursh).

In spite of my struggles with reading, I enjoyed the challenge. The first book I read in my life was *Run, Spot, Run*. Luckily, Miss Montoya allowed me to take the reader home to practice aloud on my own with one major drawback. If I made any mistakes—which I undoubtedly did—there was no one to correct me. My father, as mentioned earlier, dropped out of school in the fifth grade and was of little help since English for him was nonexistent. Mom was worse off given that she never attended a day of school in her life.

After some tutoring in class by the older students, the day soon came when the first graders and I were asked to read in front of the class. Thinking that I was ready, I eagerly raised my hand. I was prepared to show off my reading skills.

"Bueno, Nasario. ¿Estás listo?" (Are you ready?) Miss Montoya asked.

"¡Listo!" I responded, exhibiting utmost confidence. I stood proudly in front of the class with the book firmly in both hands, and I began. "*Rrun, Espot, Rrun.*"

"No, no, hijito. That sounds too *rrough*!" Miss Montoya exclaimed as if to imitate the trilling of my rs, but with a good-natured smile. "You must soften the r. Okay, say the following words but without rolling your r's. Ready? Repeat after me: Robert ran rapidly after Rebecca's rabbit."

I did just as she instructed me, but not without some difficulty. The rest of the first graders, at Miss Montoya's behest, repeated the same ditty. Little by little my classmates and I eased in transitioning from Spanish to English not only in the pronunciation of the letters *r* and *s* but phonetically in general. Irrespective of Miss Montoya's encouragement and help from the upper grades, reading and speaking posed formidable challenges for rural students like me at La Mesa School.

Other subjects such as art and arithmetic gradually came into play. My talents as an artist were rather limited, to say the least. I tended to draw horses with one leg shorter than the others or their ears came out too long. Math was a different story. I enjoyed memorizing the multiplication tables and reciting them in front of the class, although I was puzzled to learn that $2 + 2$ and 2×2 rendered the same answer. Somehow 4 in both instances didn't make sense to me. Even so, such recitation helped me and everyone else in the pronunciation of English though not appreciably.

But reciting our multiplication tables was only part of our daily exercises. Next Miss Montoya asked two or three third or fourth graders to go to the blackboard. She gave each one a math problem to solve. Everyone at their desks wrote down answers to the same problems, including the upper grades. Miss Montoya provided the correct answers so that each student could check his or her answers for correctness.

A few minutes later Miss Montoya asked Emilia, a seventh grader, to go to the blackboard. Supposedly a whiz in math, she was to serve as a model for the younger students. As Emilia walked down the middle of the classroom, someone took aim with a rubber band as a shooter and hit her in the butt with a *tetón*, a green pod. A loud "¡Ay!" (Ouch!), erupted. An irritated Emilia looked around. Nobody laughed.

Miss Montoya immediately saw the missile that landed on the floor. "Vamos a ver. ¿Quién es el malcriao?" (Let's see. Who's the wise guy?). There was dead silence. "There is a saying in Spanish that I learned from my grandfather," she continued. "It goes like this. 'Por los pecados diuno pagan todos.' (Because of the sins of one bad apple [a bad person] everyone else bears the punishment.) I'll ask one time and no more. Who hit Emilia in the *nalga*?" Still there was dead silence. "Was he a third grader or a fourth grader? Or was he a fifth grader?" "Yes!" sounded a core of female voices. "Very well, will the wise guy please stand," but nobody stood up. "In that case, I want all fifth-grade boys to stand in front of the class with their tongues sticking out. You will remain that way until the *malcriao* [brat] sticks his tongue back in his mouth. Is that clear?"

Perhaps feeling a sense of embarrassment more than guilt, a shy chubby boy admitted his indiscretion. That taught him, the rest of the fifth-grade boys, and the entire class, above all the boys, not to be a cutup in class or to be disrespectful of one another.

Before long, it was Christmas vacation. To get into the holiday spirit, Miss Montoya introduced us to several English Christmastime songs. Though the lyrics were different, the melodies were familiar to me. One popular song was "Vamos todos a Belén" (Let Us All Go to Bethlehem) because it's a song I learned from Grandma Lale, my paternal grandmother who sang it in her church choir in our village of Ojo del Padre. I still recall the first stanza:

Vamos todos a Belén,	Let us go to Bethlehem,
con amor y gozo.	with love and joy.
Adoremos al Señor,	Let us pray to our Lord
nuestro Redentor.	Jesus Christ our Redeemer.

Another Christmas carol that was eminently popular in our village was "Noche de paz" (Oh, Peaceful Night), sometimes translated as "Silent Night," but the words in English differed somewhat. Here in Spanish and English are the words to the first stanza:

Noche de amor,	Oh, peaceful night,
noche de paz.	oh, peaceful night.
Todos duermen,	Everyone's asleep,
en rededor.	here and there.

After we finished this last song, Miss Montoya asked if anyone knew a song we wanted to share with the class. She paused for a moment and waited for a response. No one answered. Finally, my cousin Juan raised his hand. "Yes, Juan, do you have a song for us?" she asked.

"Yes. I would like to ask my cousin Nasario to join me in singing 'Bendito, Bendito,'" he responded in Spanish.

"Bueno, canten" (Okay, sing), added Miss Montoya. I cleared my throat, and Juan and I sang the first words to another one of Grandma Lale's Christmas carols.

Bendito, bendito,	Blessed, oh, blessed,
bendito sea Dios.	oh, blessed, oh, Lord.
Los ángeles cantan,	The angels are singing
y alaban a Dios.	and praising God.
Los ángeles cantan,	The angels are singing
y alaban a Dios.	and praising God.

As soon as Juan and I began to sing the rest of our classmates chimed in. They also knew the words. Miss Montoya cracked a big smile.

She taught us one new Christmas carol. "Jingle Bells," whose words she wrote in large letters on the blackboard. First, we repeated the lyrics after her and then she sang the song. The boys sang the words to the chorus.

Dashing through the snow,
on a one horse open sleigh,
o'er the fields we go,
laughing all the way.
Bells on bob tails ring
making spirits bright,
oh what fun it is to laugh and sing
a sleighing song tonight.

Chorus
Jingle bells, jingle bells,
jingle all the way.
Oh what fun it is to ride
on a one horse open sleigh, eigh!

Judging from the initial enthusiasm, the class liked the new song (I did, too), but Miss Montoya paused and warned some of the mischievous boys that the words were "jingle bells," not "*chingo* bells" (screw the bells). Everybody burst out laughing. The new song and melody certainly added to everyone's joy. Of course some of us still had our own pronunciation problems of certain words (e.g., snow > esnow; way > guey).

After Christmas vacation, school resumed. We quickly adapted to the daily routine that varied very little from the fall term, with one or two exceptions. The older boys were now kept busy feeding the potbelly wood stove to warm the classroom. Because of the cold winter, recess was confined to the classroom except for those students who had to use the outhouse or the hardy souls who could tolerate the freezing temperatures outdoors. Most of the lower grades—both girls and boys—stayed inside.

The rest of the year was quite repetitive if not humdrum. Miss Montoya followed what impressed me as a fairly standard schedule that on paper showed progression, but not necessarily improvement among her students. The majority of us continued to wrestle with the omnipresent problems of speaking and reading in English. In that sense, progress as a whole was microscopic at best.

My first school year ended without much fanfare. Not having English reading, writing, or speaking assignments to contend with in the summer was a welcome relief. I was just as elated as my classmates. I looked forward to working on the ranch. We said goodbye to Miss Montoya. I would miss her, being that she was exceedingly patient—just like my mother—in her teaching ways.

I performed a multitude of chores on the ranch. They included tending to my rabbits, feeding Mom's chickens, watering my horses Bayito and El Prieto, milking Dad's cows, and working in the cornfields. I also helped Mom on washdays (Mondays). The foregoing tasks were a dramatic departure from and the antithesis of reading *Run, Spot, Run* or reciting multiplication tables.

But whatever little English I learned during the school year, it came in handy when my parents and I ventured to Bernalillo north of Albuquerque. There they did their grocery shopping at the Bernalillo Mercantile Company (BMC). Though my parents were both illiterate in English they shopped for the most part by looking at pictures on canned goods or with assistance from the store owner. This was also true of most ranchers and farmers from the Río Puerco Valley where we lived.

Now with one year of schooling behind me, I was able to help Mom and Dad in translating some of the labels as they paced up and down the food aisles. My father in particular, for whatever reason, knew that some brands were more expensive than others. Del Monte products, for example, were at the top of his list, followed by

Stokely's and Libby's canned goods, the cheaper ones. At some point the forgoing comparisons prompted a question. "Dad, if Del Monte peaches cost more, how come you buy them?" I asked, somewhat puzzled. "Because they come from the mountain," he responded tongue in cheek, although I detected that it was only to show that he could recognize a word here and there in Spanish.

Most of the canned products that we bought were Libby's. They included Libby's Vienna Sausages (*choricitos*) and Libby's Corned Beef; both were very popular in my family. Mom would peel and dice potatoes, cut small bits of white onions, and fry both ingredients in a pan with a can of corned beef for supper. The sausages were excellent for packing in saddles bags for a quick snack rolled in a flour tortilla. Dad and I did this under the shade of a juniper tree whenever we went for firewood in the monte woods during the summer, or on the open range for cattle roundups either in the spring or the fall.

Before long, my second year of school was about to begin. I was excited to return to La Mesa School in Rincón del Cochino. At first glance, the start of a new school year compared to my first-grade experiences, was anticlimactic, with one noticeable difference. We now had a new teacher, Miss Evangelina Baca from Peña Blanca south of Santa Fe. I have no idea what happened to Miss Montoya. I missed her but I, like the rest of the students, soon adapted to Miss Baca.

Like Miss Montoya, Miss Baca looked just as young as one or two of the eighth graders. During World War II, according to Miss Baca in an interview I conducted with her on October 4, 1980, in Albuquerque, "Many teachers were hired to teach right after having graduated from high school. Other teachers were hired with just nine or ten college hours. Qualifications were very modest because teachers were in high demand."

I noticed one other thing as the new school started—a slight depletion in student population. As Miss Baca reiterated in our interview, "I had no first grade, no sixth grade, and no seventh grade." Yet the Valencias, Jorge and Melecia where Miss Baca boarded, provided at least five of the students' total enrollment: Vangie, Ocariz, Villa, Tony, and Edwina.

Like the rest of the students, bit by bit I became accustomed to Miss Baca's teaching methodology that varied little from her predecessor. She also had her heart in teaching and was a good role model for students. Her words of encouragement and discouragement when I interviewed her spoke volumes. "I was very happy. The children were very good. The parents treated me with such respect. I was a paragon of knowledge in their eyes. All of that esteem and respect that parents and children had for teachers is gone forever, now."

The challenges Miss Baca and her students faced did not vary one iota from those in my first year of schooling. The problems with English, whether in speaking, writing, or reading, were still unmistakable. Though the textbooks were all in English, she employed Spanish on occasion to ease the pressure with seemingly little success as the school year progressed. English aside, the lack of class time and having multiple grades were a double-edged sword for Miss Baca. "Having enough time," she reiterated in the aforementioned interview, "was always the problem in teaching so many grades. I felt that one advantage was the pupils would listen to what I was teaching and, even if they were in a grade below or above the grade I was teaching, they would hear something taught many times over in a one-room school."

Devoted teachers without doubt derived their own personal satisfaction from teaching, because the salaries Sandoval County of New Mexico paid were meager, according to Miss Baca. She informed me that her salary for the 1944–1945 school year was $80 per month, that is, $960 total for the entire calendar year. From her monthly income she paid the Valencias room and board. She also spent her own money to purchase paper and other school supplies because the state's school budget was inadequate. (That regrettably is still true today among many public-school teachers.)

Soon the school year was over, and so too was Miss Baca's tenure at La Mesa School in Rincón del Cochino. She was not to return, and neither would I.

Threatening droughts struck with a vengeance. Living off the land became a losing proposition. To make matters worse, my father's employment with the WPA (Works Progress Administration) and CCC camps, two venerable programs under Franklin D. Roosevelt, had also come to an abrupt end. Living on the fringes and struggling to provide the basic necessities for a growing family became exceedingly difficult. My concerned parents took stock of our lives in this moment, but the gloom confronting them also plagued other farmers and ranchers of the Río Puerco Valley.

In July 1945, my parents made the bold move to an unfamiliar place called the Santa Barbara/Martíneztown neighborhood in Albuquerque. A new home, a new vicinity, and a new school awaited me and my family. Our immediate future hung in the balance.

The Santa Barbara/Martíneztown
Nightmare

IN JULY 1945, JUST PRIOR to the end of World War II, my father—like countless other ranchers and farmers in the Río Puerco Valley where he was born—was no longer able to live off the land to feed the family on my paternal grandparents' ranch where we lived. The skies had become increasingly frugal with their clouds and precipitation. Dry farming (*de temporal*) had reached a low ebb, and a defining moment was at hand.

Our past was clear, our present very much in the balance, and our future as muddy as the Río Puerco waters close to our casita east of the San Mateo Mountains (today called Mount Taylor) where I spent the formative years of my life.

Hoping for a better life Mom and Dad decided to move the family to Albuquerque (they always pronounced it Alburquerque, like our sister city in Spain). In Dad's old Chevrolet (carrito), we loaded our precious belongings: clothing, bedding, dishes, utensils, pots and pans, and whatever food we had at our disposal. My dog Chopo, who was part of the family, came along. A new and strange place awaited us.

The summer morning was relatively cool as we said *adiós* to our two-room casita at the ranch. Our new dwelling would be at my paternal grandparents' property in so-called Martíneztown, a historic Hispanic enclave in what was then northeast Albuquerque. Their home, which they bought in 1912, the year my father was born at the ranch, was actually in Santa Barbara, an area north of Martíneztown and west of the historic Santa Barbara Cemetery. Most local residents considered Santa Barbara an integral part of Martíneztown. My grandpa and grandma's home was at 417 Wilson Avenue, an unlikely name in a Hispanic neighborhood, but this was not to be the only anomaly. There would be others in the foreseeable future.

By the time we arrived in Martíneztown, the afternoon was muggy and hot. My two youngest brothers and two little sisters were tired, cranky, and hungry. I was in no better mood. Our first meal in unfamiliar surroundings consisted of cold tortillas, *chicharrones*, *carne seca* (jerky), and rice pudding that Mom had packed in a Mason jar. Our hunger pangs fast disappeared, but the new and stifling environment conjured up thoughts of uncertainty and apprehension.

Beltrán, my six-year-old brother, with a penchant for cutting up even as a small boy, was the first to react. "¿Aquí vamos a vivir en este cuarto toos atoraos? ¡Está más chiquito que tu gallinero, amá!" (Is this the room where we're going to live all cramped up? Mom, it's smaller than your chicken coop!) Mom, sensing more than a modicum of reality to Beltrán's innocent words, didn't respond. He had said a mouthful.

My parents, four siblings, and I suddenly found ourselves in Grandma's storage room (*dispensa*) located in the backyard, packed like sheep. My sister Terry was born in the storage room two years later, July 14, 1947. Our new so-called home, nestled within the city boundaries, was about the size of our family bedroom at the ranch. As you entered, there was a small window to the right of the door that provided a bit of natural light. A small wood-burning stove stood near the door as one entered, the only entrance available. Next to the stove there was a small *trastero* (cupboard), from whence *cucarachas* (disgusting brown cockroaches) crawled out every morning when I fetched a bowl for my oatmeal. A small dining table and four chairs complemented the tiny kitchen area. My parents' bed was toward the back of the room. Unbeknownst to me and the rest of the family, Grandma's storage room would be our home for the next four long and unforgettable years (1945–1949).

Paradoxically, Grandma lived alone on the same lot in a four-room house with a porch (*portal*). She, too, due to the forces of nature on the farm, was compelled to live in Martíneztown year-round, much to her delight since now in her golden years she favored the city over rural life. Grandpa on the other hand, was a diehard rancher-farmer who preferred to live in the countryside until he, too, like his fellow ranchers and farmers, was forced to abandon the Río Puerco Valley. Furthermore, he was in his 80s and losing his eyesight as well as his hearing.

Regardless of the seeming bleakness of life in Martíneztown, a few things were quite familiar to me. First of all, visible to the naked eye in the barrio (neighborhood) was an outhouse (escusao) in every household. Secondly, women hung their clothes out to dry on clotheslines on Mondays, wash day. And thirdly, the stove pipe chimneys spewed plumes of light and dark smoke from the wood-burning stoves.

Familiar, too, were poor, proud, and hardworking men and women who long ago had settled in the neighborhood. Plus they all spoke Spanish. A few knew a little English, although their children and grandchildren fared a tad better.

My family enjoyed, in a manner of speaking, some conveniences such as electricity. We had a light bulb with an electrical cord that hung from the ceiling in the middle of our one-room dwelling. This was our main source of light in addition to a kerosene lamp that we used sparingly to save money on oil. Pumping water from my grandmother's well was also a novelty to me. There would be additional discoveries, some pleasant, others not, as life in Martíneztown unfolded for me and my family in the coming months and years.

Year by year Mom became increasingly jittery in our cramped quarters. My father did his best to console her. "Nothing lasts forever, *m'hija* [my dear]," he averred. He promised her that one day we would have our own home where she could spread her wings and once again feel the same sense of freedom she had enjoyed in the open spaces back in the Río Puerco Valley.

For me, a boy nine years old, the unlimited space I had enjoyed in the countryside was now reduced to square footage. Half of my grandparents' property was enclosed by a wooden fence; the other half was a barbed wire fence. I could even reach across the rag-tag wire fence and touch the walls of the neighbor's house that was plastered with cement instead of mud.

Standing in the middle of Wilson Avenue, I could eye the dirt road and the houses up and down the street, one lined up after the other. They struck me as chickens roosting in their chicken coop.

For the time being, we endured in our tiny habitat. During the winter my two youngest sisters Elsie and Terry slept with my parents, and my oldest sister Julia went under their bed. As for me the eldest of my siblings, I had the privilege of sleeping on a folding cot whereas my two brothers, Beltrán and Juanito, slept underneath me in a makeshift bed. Every evening we brought in the cot from the carport adjacent to our dwelling, and every morning we folded it and took it back out.

All through the summer, unless we were at the ranch, two of us slept in Dad's car. Beltrán, three years younger than me, slept in the front seat with his feet under the steering wheel. I spent the night in the more spacious back seat.

Whether summer, winter, spring or fall, the sleeping arrangements were hardly chaotic. Each one of us knew his or her role, and the routine was carried out with utter precision, a reflection of my father's methodical way of doing things. His folk saying, "Haz las cosas al revés y las haces otra vez." (Do things helter-skelter, and you'll do them again.)

Though life can be adventurous when you're a kid, I found our new modus vivendi abnormal and tiring. The strangeness I felt at times was overbearing. Not only did I have to learn the meaning and implications of the word barrio, but I also quickly discovered that the local community did not readily embrace newcomers. We felt like strangers from another land.

My first eye-opening experience occurred at Santa Barbara School about three blocks from where we lived. To go from second grade in a one-room adobe schoolhouse with multiple grades—first through eighth—to an urban, cement-plastered school where a single third-grade class held twenty-five to thirty pupils was a surprise. Although most of my classmates were Hispanic, some of them even had Anglo surnames (e.g., Sprunk). Two or three Anglos and a Black, or Negroes as they were called back then, added to the ethnic mix.

A number of Hispanics acted as if they spoke only English, but in time I realized that they had their own linguistic problems. English for some of them was only marginally better than mine, but speaking or reading in English, indeed a foreign language for me, was compounded because of the perpetual interference from Spanish. The *ch*'s became *sh*'s (church > *shursh*), and the letter *v* turned into *b* (very > bery), and so on. These linguistic nuances or idiosyncrasies were nothing new. I had experienced them at La Mesa School in Rincón del Cochino in the Río Puerco Valley.

Aside from personally laboring with English, there were social issues I had to contend with, especially as regard to my Hispanic classmates. Instead of extending a cordial welcome as one of their own, for the most part they were aloof and even heartless. They made fun of my high-top shoes, long-sleeve white shirt, and bib overalls. I stood out like a sore thumb and so was a prime target for their ridicule.

To my Hispanic compatriots I was just another *serreño*, a country bumpkin who hailed from Tajique or Carnuel (situated in the Manzano Mountains east of Albuquerque). They invoked these two place names that meant nothing to me, and maybe even less so to them. Yet they delighted in poking fun at outsiders. Such taunting was tantamount to bullying, the popular jargon among kids nowadays.

Every day after school, I changed into my playing or work clothes to chop wood for Mom's small wood-burning stove. Though I wore the same clothes to school virtually every day, they were clean. Mom made sure of that. Still, kids made snide remarks under their breath about my hygiene. "¡A la veca! ¡Ese vato sí que huele!" (Holy shit! That dude sure does stink!) At first I didn't quite comprehend their mumbo jumbo, but I presumed that it wasn't very nice. I ignored their gibberish and endured the agony as long as I could before telling Mom. When I finally did, she was much more understanding than Dad. "Hazte el sordo, hijito" (Pretend not to hear them, my dear son), Mom said. Dad, on the other hand, was less sympathetic. He thought the kids' teasing was nothing out of the ordinary.

My father, a very intelligent man with only a fifth-grade education and no technical skills whatsoever, had found a job at the Wool Warehouse Company on North First Street away from downtown Albuquerque. There he unloaded, sorted, and stacked cowhides and sheepskins brought to town by ranchers and sheep farmers from the countryside, including the Río Puerco Valley. It was hard work, and he had little spare time for kids' stuff.

My third-grade teacher who shall remain anonymous didn't help matters one iota either. She was known as a mean-old goat. Students maintained that her meanness stemmed from having a wooden leg, which made her walk with a limp. Some kids had the gall to mimic her walk and even wished that termites somehow would infest her wooden leg. She did not enjoy a decent rapport with her students and because of that did not have a good reputation as teacher.

After about three weeks of endless agony, I hated the kids and my teacher. I detested school and wanted to quit. The straw that broke the camel's back, as it were, occurred on the playground. This boy with jet-black hair parted down the middle came up to me at recess and pretended to be friendly. "¡Órale!" (Hey dude!) he said, an expression, like some of the other gobbledygook city kids employed, I didn't quite grasp. "You *guant* to play bingo?"

"¿Qué es eso?" (What's that?) I asked innocently.

"Tú te enpinas y yo te chingo" (You bend over and I'll screw you), he replied, and he laughed aloud. I understood what the vulgar phrase meant. Two or three kids who were eves dropping, a girl among them, burst out laughing as well. I felt a gut-wrenching blow to the pit of my stomach. I wanted to beat the crap out of him (darle una buena turra) but knew I would get in trouble. Instead, I went home crying once school was over.

"¿Qué te pasa hijito?" (What's wrong?) my mother asked as I walked in our one-room house. Amid sobs I told her the whole story. She listened intently and sympathized with me.

At the dinner table, she informed my father about the kids' goading. Though a bit more sympathetic this time, his reaction was quite predictable. "Víbora que chilla, no pica" (A hissing rattlesnake doesn't bite), he exclaimed as he looked askance. His words were hardly comforting or reassuring. After all, I was the one being pestered.

As Mom and I looked at each other, my brothers and sisters ate in shifts at the tiny dinner table that seated four. She seemed to be asking in silence, "What have we gotten ourselves into by moving here?" I could tell she was worried.

Away from school the situation was hardly better. Some of the neighbors spurned us; others were suspiciously friendly. Even the dogs sensed that we were strangers. I came home from school one Friday afternoon, but Chopo was not at Grandma's front yard to greet me as he customarily did. I walked in the house. Before I could ask Mom of his whereabouts, she said to me with a disheartened look. "Hijito, you better go see Chopo." Immediately I sensed that something was wrong. I ran out the door and found him lying listless on the ground in front of Dad's car. Seeing me, he let out a faint groan and then closed his eyes. He never woke up. I felt a profound and hurt feeling. I had lost a dear friend.

I went back in the house. Mom was sitting in a chair next to the stove holding my baby sister Mary Elsie in her arms. Mom looked at me. I looked at her. "Amá," I said to her in a quivering voice. "Aquí ni los perros nos quieren." (Not even the dogs like us here.)

Chopo liked to follow me to school. Over and over again I had to say, "Chopo, a casa, a casa." (Go on home, go on home.) That Friday morning he followed me for a short distance. He then turned around and headed home. I then heard a commotion from afar, but I never suspected that Chopo was involved in the fracas. Somehow he managed to get home with his ears and legs mangled. His face was in no better shape. I was angry.

On Saturday morning Dad and I took him to a burial site for pets east of present-day Interstate 25 and Indian School Road. Dad looked at my forlorn face and said, "Even animals deserve a decent burial. We're not going to bury him here surrounded by heaps of garbage and trash. We'll bury him at the ranch where he was born," and that's what we did over the weekend. When we left the burial site next to Mom's chicken coop, I felt a deep, empty feeling and vowed never to own a dog ever again—and I didn't.

Bit by bit my family and I adjusted to the quasi-urban community. Neighbors began to act more civil. Even my grandmother, whom I sensed saw us as intruders, remained somewhat aloof, but gradually she warmed up to us. I ran errands for her to Felipe García's Grocery Store (no relation) on Edith Boulevard (the historic house still stands). I bought meat, sugar, and butter for her using red and blue World War II ration tokens. Other times she sent me to a smaller store at Wilson Avenue and Broadway owned by a pint-sized man with spectacles named Carlos Buenas.

My father's job at the Wool Warehouse Company started out well. He walked the four-mile roundtrip daily to save on bus fare.

Though he was paid a paltry sum, he and Mom managed to make ends meet and even saved a little money in the process. Dad's main wish was to buy a truck for ranch work and to haul some of his calves and steers to market at the stockyards in south Albuquerque. His second wish was to save enough money to buy a piece of property on which to build Mom a house.

For the time being both dreams appeared elusive. After less than a year, my father was laid off at Wool Warehouse Company. I often heard him say, "No hay que estar ahi con los brazos crusaos esperando el bien de Dios." (One can't sit around with folded arms waiting for God's will.) In other words, "Get off your butt and do something." Dad walked two doors up the street (Hutchinson Fruit Company was next door to Wool Warehouse Company) to where Crane O'Fallon Company was located. He inquired about a job, was hired, and worked there performing a variety of chores, among them unloading pipe and plumbing fixtures from railroad cars. He was employed at Crane from 1946 until he retired as warehouse manager in 1974.

In Martíneztown I made friends. Among them were Lauro "Loro" Crespín from San Ysidro, west of Jémez Pueblo, who lived next door to Santa Barbara School (we're still friends), and Pat Perea whose father owned Mike's Paint and Body Shop a few houses down the street from where we lived. I worked there an hour or two after school. I swept and cleaned the garages and washed cars. I earned from ten up to fifteen cents an hour. On weekends I made more money. I sanded cars' fenders prior to being sprayed with a coat of prime paint. After the primer dried, I sanded the fenders once again before Pat's uncle applied the final coat of paint. My job was hard work and dirty, but the earnings helped me buy pencils, tablets, and other school supplies. Throughout the summer I earned more money. That being so, on Sundays I treated the entire family to popsicles or Eskimo pies. They were refreshing and a novelty for all of us.

For breakfast Mom prepared scrambled eggs or oatmeal that we were accustomed to, but in addition I ate Kellogg's Corn Flakes. Since we had no refrigerator to store fresh milk, I mixed the cereal with coffee, which was ghastly. During the winter my parents bought Carnation canned milk because it was not apt to turn sour (I found the label on the can rather humorous since it boasted that the milk came from contented cows.).

Aside from the traditional beans and chile or meat and potatoes concoctions, flour tortillas decked the dinner table. Mom also fried ring baloney with fried potatoes. Canned salmon or Spam that my parents had discovered long ago at the Bernalillo Mercantile Company (BMC) appeared at dinnertime as well. After my brothers Beltrán, Juanito, and I nagged our parents about being tired of tortillas, Rainbow Bread found its way onto the dinner table. But beans and chile remained our main staples year-round. Except for hamburger meat (*carne molida*), baloney, and chicken that Mom cooked on occasion, we ate very little meat. This was the antithesis of our meat diet at the ranch where we ate a variety of meats year-round including fried rabbit.

Somehow we survived the first nine months in Albuquerque. In June Mom, my siblings and I headed to the ranch for the summer to take care of our house (e.g., mud plaster), tend to farm chores, and to take care of our farm animals. I was glad to reacquaint myself with my two steeds, Bayito and El Prieto. My father worked weekdays, but he visited us on weekends. The summer months at the farm were a great psychological boost for the entire family. Mom in particular could sing her favorites song without concern of disturbing the neighbors. In August we returned to Albuquerque, but now we did not come as country bumpkins or total strangers. Things were better. We had paid our dues, in a manner of speaking.

My second year at Santa Barbara School was by far more pleasant. My fourth-grade teacher was a Padilla just like my paternal grandmother (Emilia Padilla) before she married Grandpa. It was a name I could relate to. Miss Padilla spoke Spanish and English so she helped me with my English, which still gave me fits. She was very nice. Because of her, I became more enthusiastic about my schoolwork, but that was short-lived.

My admiration for my fifth- and sixth-grade teachers as well as my interest in classwork slowly waned. After two or three of us finished our assignments early with idle time on our hands, we talked to each other or to other classmates. As a consequence, and minus any forewarning from the teachers, I spent an inordinate amount of time in one corner or the other facing the wall in front of the classroom. There I sat. But there's more. For talking in class (usually out of boredom) my punishment was to write hundreds if not thousands of times inane phrases in yellow tablets such as "I will not talk in class" or "I will not ever, ever talk in class again." At times I completed tablet upon tablet replete with that mindless wordiness. This was particularly true in our rowdy sixth-grade class, but I was not alone. Two or three other kids endured the same punishment. To add to the indignity, the teacher did not provide the tablets. Because of that I had to spend some of the money I earned at Perea's Paint and Body Shop to purchase them.

The harsh treatment accorded me and other boys (not the girls) was not only demeaning but pointless. Regardless of the circumstances or parties involved, from my vantage point there were no winners, neither the teachers nor the students.

Reflecting on the past, I now realize that my fifth- and sixth-grade teachers like countless of my future public school teachers were not exceedingly creative or progressive. If students finished their assignments with time to spare, they neither challenged you intellectually nor did they reward you with special assignments such as reading privileges in the school library. Instead, punishment superseded encouragement.

But let me be fair. I and other students were no angels. As naïve as I was back then, I thought that public school teachers were overloaded with too many classes and students to teach. In addition to their teaching responsibilities, they had other duties (e.g., supervising study hall). Some teachers even fell asleep at their desk at lunchtime. Teaching at times took its toll.

Seventy years later, my opinion with regard to teachers being overworked—and even underpaid—remains unchanged. They are, after all, the yeomen and yeowomen in the trenches; they are the ones who make the difference between success or failure of students after they graduate from high school. To state it differently, the future of students' well-being is predicated on inspiration and good quality education in the public schools.

The school bell rang; it was time for the morning recess. My schoolmates and I headed outdoors where a bulky kid was hitting fly balls to the outfield for three or four kids to catch. I was fascinated to see how such a husky boy could hit a ball so far out and high up in the air.

As I watched, this blonde girl came up to me and started to talk. "Hi! Yo soy Dorotea. I'm in the same class with you," she said.

"Yes, I've seen you but I thought you were . . . "

"But you thought I was a *gringa*, huh!" Dorotea interrupted with a slight grin before I could finish my sentence. "Don't worry. I won't hold that against you . . . and by the way, I don't think the teacher has been very kind to you. And something else, if she punished me the way she does you, I would cry."

"Well, I'm not one to cry," I responded.

"And why not?" she queried.

"Porque los hombres no lloran" (Because men don't cry), I said, recalling my maternal grandmother's words in Bernalillo with whom I sometimes spent time. It was her way of saying, "Be strong."

That afternoon I had a different kind of an encounter on the playground with two boys who were in my sixth-grade class. "¡Órale, carnal! [Hey, bro!] I'm Rico," spouted one of them. "We saw you talking to la Dora this morning. ¡Wáchala! (Look out for her!). She can give you the *chingas* (a good fuck)."

"Yeaaaah. She screeeews really goo, goo, good," added the second kid who seemed to stutter.

"And do you know how I know," continued Rico, "'cause some wise guy wrote a poem 'bout her giving him *craques* [having sex]. You wanna hear it?"

Without waiting for a response, he proceeded to recite the poem:

One, we started to have fun.
Two, I asked her for a screw.
Three, she gave it to me free.
Four, I laid her on the floor.
Five, she said she wanted more.
Six, she started to get sick.
Seven, she thought she was in heaven.
Eight, the doctor was at the gate.
Nine, she said she was just fine.
Ten, we started all over again.

Rico had barely finished reciting the verses when the bell rang. Like countless other inanities at school, I didn't think his poetics were very kind.

Throughout my four years in Martíneztown, I learned as much on the streets as I did in the classroom. Respect, obedience, and caring for your neighbor took on a different meaning from what I had been taught at home in rural New Mexico. Whereas my parents clung to their old customs and traditions, Martíneztown somehow seemed to embody values antithetical to those of my own upbringing.

Drunken sprees on weekends, domestic violence, and petty

crimes plagued the barrio, but family weddings and a drink or two among honorable compadres also comprised the festive and not-so-festive environment. Because my parents believed in our culture, and I believed in them, my siblings and I abided by their rules and principles.

Ever since we arrived in Albuquerque, I had wondered if a different world existed away from Santa Barbara School and Martíneztown. As I intermingled with kids from my street such as Danny Seiler whose father was in the military, Louie Córdova who lived caddy corner from Grandma's house, and Pat Perea, mentioned earlier, I became more and more familiarized with places away from Wilson Avenue where I lived.

Pat's family owned a dump truck for hauling junk to raw property they owned (today this Albuquerque land forms part of Interstate 25 and Indian School Road). What's more, in the summer the truck was used to haul kindling and scraps of lumber given away at the sawmill north of historic Old Town. The Pereas used both for their wood stoves in the three households they maintained. Winter trips to the saw mill did not abate. The joy of riding in the back of the dump truck loaded with firewood—plus getting paid a few nickels for unloading it—added to my youthful and ever-expanding experiences in Albuquerque.

Another episode that looms for me is my first movie at the long-defunct La Mesa Theatre on Central Avenue. The Sunday prior to Ash Wednesday, I heard a knock at the screen door of our one-room dwelling. "Go see who it is," said Mom. It was Pat Perea and two other kids. "Hey!" said Pat. "You wanna go to the *mono* with us?" "And what's a mono?" I countered. "The movies," chimed in one of the other boys. "But I'll have to ask my father if I can go," I responded.

After a brief discussion between Mom and Dad, he told the boys I could go but cautioned us not to get into any trouble. He asked how much the movies cost. "Twenty-five cents," said Pat without hesitation. Five cents for the movies, ten cents for a soft drink and popcorn, plus ten cents for the bus fare." From the small leather coin purse that Dad customarily carried in the right front pocket of his Levi's, he fetched three nickels and gave them to me to pay for the movies and the treats. "Dad, what about the bus fare?" His answer was straight and to the point: "Walk!" And walk we did.

Evidently going to the movies was something Pat and his friends did routinely. I had but a vague idea what movies were about. Boy was I in for a startling surprise.

Walking to and from the movies in downtown Albuquerque, roughly five to six miles roundtrip, proved exciting. Pat and his buddies knew the way—including shortcuts. We maneuvered our way south on Broadway, crisscrossed the railroads tracks, and traversed back roads and alleys. We reached La Mesa Theatre where many inner-city kids evidently went on Sunday afternoons (the city's other movie theater, El Rey, also on Central Avenue at the present time is a nightclub). The second feature was about to start. We stumbled in semi-darkness for seats at the very front of the theater. By then the Looney Tunes cartoons were showing on the large screen. I had never in my life seen anything as eye-catching and colorful.

When the regular feature started, starring Red Ryder and Little Beaver, I saw the galloping horses on the huge screen headed for us in the front row. I thought we were going to be trampled to death. Having been raised around horses, I had an unmistakable understanding of the damage they could incur on the human body. So, I ducked to one side and hit the floor. Everybody around me, including Pat Perea and his friends, burst out laughing. By now I was presumably among friends and as a result did not let their teasing bother me.

Nibbling on popcorn and sipping a soft drink as we watched the film, too, was totally new to me. I was having a ball. Our trip back home turned out to be terrific as well because with the money Pat and his pals saved on bus fare, they bought plenty of candy to eat along the way. I loved the chewy Tootsie-Rolls and Big Hunk Candy Bar. I had never eaten either one before.

My first movie was an unforgettable experience. I could hardly wait to get home to share my excitement with Mom, even though I was certain she wouldn't quite comprehend everything since she had never been to a movie herself. After my first trip to a movie outside the confines of Santa Barbara and Martíneztown, I felt a tad wiser. That afternoon I thought I had matured. Little did I realize that I had much more to learn right in Grandma's back yard.

Easter Sunday had arrived. On this special day Mom, without fail, made sure we children looked our very best, above all, the girls. That week she had bought new dresses for my little sisters Julianita and Mary Elsie. While she dressed them in their new outfits, I ventured to Felipe García's store and bought orange and banana popsicles for the family. I gave each of my sisters one. Then they went and sat at the doorsteps to Grandma's kitchen to enjoy the treat. As they were licking and savoring their popsicles, Grandma who tended to be grumpy—presumably without seeing my sisters who were sitting outside her door—tossed a pan of dirty dishwater through the kitchen's screen door.

My sisters with their white dresses drenched and soiled, went crying to Mom. She was very hurt and angry at what she perceived to be Grandma's deliberate act. At that very moment, and without mincing her words, Mom said to Dad. "We're moving! And the sooner the better! Ya basta. Ya estoy cansada de todo este martirio en esta vecindá. [Enough is enough. I'm tired of all the suffering in this neighborhood.]"

And move we did after school ended at Santa Barbara for my two younger brothers and me. Without wasting anytime, and at my mother's insistence, we packed our belongings and left for our new dwelling in Los Ranchos de Alburquerque approximately eight miles north of the city.

Amid bumps and bruises, four long tumultuous years at Martíneztown had taught me a multitude of things both in and outside the classroom. Despite a veritable nightmare, my family and I survived the trials and tribulations in semi-urban Albuquerque. Throughout the ordeal my parents taught me, in particular my mother, that when survival is at stake, there is no substitute for the human spirit.

A Hop, Skip, and a Jump

THE FATEFUL TIME TO ABANDON Martíneztown occurred in June 1949 when, much to Mom's relief and happiness, we moved into our two-room adobe house in historic Los Ranchos de Alburquerque. My parents had saved enough money to purchase a quarter-acre plot from Daniel Sedillo who, coincidentally, hailed from Martíneztown but now lived in Los Ranchos, two houses away from our new home.

When we relocated to what Mom called her Casa Alegre "Happy Home," it was barely finished. The outside walls still needed to be mud plastered although the inside was mud plastered and white washed. Dad had painstakingly built the home on weekends and holidays with adobe bricks that he and I hauled from Martíneztown. In fact, the forlorn lot on Edith Boulevard south of Mountain Road where the adobe bricks were made and sundried is still there.

Our new residence for a family of eight (two parents and six children), with two more kids born later, was still inadequate, but it was a vast improvement over Grandma's cramped storage room. Two more adobe rooms plus a separate garage were added as we settled in Los Ranchos. This was to be the family home for the next fifty-two years until Dad, a widower, passed away in 2001 at age eighty-eight.

For the moment the size of the house was inconsequential be-cause it was Mom's house, much to her delight. Freedom was in the air, and she was thrilled. Unlike the inner city where the homes were clustered together, here in semi-rural Los Ranchos Mom could now sing her favorite Mexican songs without a concern about disturbing the neighbors. Among the songs that she learned at the ranch from listening to a battery-operated radio on Saturday mornings were beautiful ballads, "Zenaida" among them, one of her favorites. Other popular songs she sang were Mexican folk songs (*rancheras*) until that fateful day May 25, 1972, when she passed away at the age of fifty-two.

Farm-like Los Ranchos, too, was more to my liking than the inner city. A ditch ran near our house, and the *(d)renaje* (a drainage ditch) likewise was close by. But no one took advantage of the acequia, or ditch system, more than Max Chávez. Two doors down from us he planted several tracts of chile, cantaloupes, and watermelons. Come harvest time, "don Maque," as he was affectionately known to the locals, sold green chile to virtually every Hispanic household in the vicinity. People roasted the ubiquitous chile for immediate consumption, or they sun dried it for use during the winter months. *Ristras* or strings of dried red chile peppers that decorated the homes' facades were used as well throughout the winter to make red chile sauce.

These farming and harvesting activities brought to a close our first summer in Los Ranchos de Alburquerque. Now it was time to prepare for school. Mom and Dad had bought my two younger brothers and me new clothes for our debut at Los Ranchos Elementary School.

Los Ranchos Elementary School— A Pleasant Experience

The first day of school had arrived for me, Beltrán, and Juanito. Beltrán was ten years old. Juanito, the youngest of the three of us, was eight. By now I was thirteen years old and ready to start the seventh grade. Each of us had our school supplies in a small canvas-like bag which consisted of a riding tablet, pencil, a gum eraser, and a ruler. In addition, I had what was called a math compass and protractor.

Dad wished us well and left for work at Crane O'Fallon Company, his workplace for the past three years. Then it was Mom's turn. She blessed us, something she did daily, and my brothers and I departed for school.

I was particularly anxious to meet my new teacher and to learn about Los Ranchos School and the students. We crossed Second Street and walked on Los Ranchos Road until we reached Fourth Street about a quarter mile away. The school was across Fourth Street. We arrived around 8:15. A flurry of activity greeted us on the school playground. Kids were screaming and hollering; some of them were on swings or playing tether ball. Others just wandered about perhaps getting reacquainted with classmates whom they had not seen throughout the summer. Two or three teachers greeted students until the school bell rang. Everyone headed for their respective classrooms, including Beltrán. I helped Juanito find his although the assistant principal had shown Mom, my brothers, and me our rooms the week prior to registration.

After accompanying Juanito to his schoolroom, I went to mine on the second floor. I was eager to meet my new teacher, Mrs. Meyerheim. Gradually I became acquainted with her as well as my classmates. I liked her and the students. As time passed, I befriended a student who sat next to me in the back of the classroom.

For an art class assignment, he would copy pictures of animals such as the Bambi that appeared on 46 oz. cans of orange juice. His copies were indistinguishable from the originals. He was very talented with an uncanny ability to draw just about anything. As for me, I had the tendency to draw horses with asymmetrical legs notwithstanding the fact that I spent my childhood on a ranch. While he was a skillful artist, I was a whiz at math and could recite my multiplication tables backward and forward. My math skills compensated for my lack of artistic flair.

Before long, it was time for the mid-morning recess. This was the perfect opportunity to get acquainted with the schoolyard and its surroundings. Granted, Los Ranchos de Alburquerque was semi-rural, but I learned very quickly that the majority of the kids were Hispanos. A number of students were Anglos; others were of Italian or Japanese descent.

Hispanic students by and large adhered to Spanish, their home language, with a smattering of English. All too familiar to me were the ever-present linguistic difficulties cited heretofore, to wit, the interference of certain Spanish consonants in pronouncing words in English. For instance, the Spanish *ch* versus *sh* (church > shurch), the initial *s* sounded like *es* (school > eschool), or the *r* at the beginning of a word was trilled or rolled so that *rich* was pronounced *rrich*. The *v*, whether in an initial position in in the middle of a word, became *b* (very > bery; marvel > *marbel*),

Regardless of the linguistic slips of the tongue or nuances, Hispanics at Los Ranchos were more cordial than those at Santa Barbara School. They didn't pretend to flaunt their English verbal skills either on the playground or in class. Whenever a Hispanic student read aloud in class, at times with a heavy accent, nobody snickered or uttered unflattering remarks under their breath. Besides, Mrs. Meyerheim, whom I came to like and appreciate more and more as the school year progressed, did not tolerate jeering of any sort. She was strict on the one hand, but empathetic with students (all students!) due to the challenges we faced, above all Hispanics because of our problems with English.

Lunchtime came. Mom had packed a lunch for my two brothers so they ate at school, but I went home to join her. From school to my house roundtrip took about twenty minutes if I didn't tarry. Consequently, I had time to eat plus play a game or two of gin rummy with Mom. This is something we had been doing since my school days in Martíneztown although she taught me the game at the ranch in the Río Puerco Valley.

Coming and going to school alone at lunchtime gave me a sense of freedom and responsibility. I was the eldest of my siblings; therefore, my parents expected more of me as I grew older. I was to be a role model for my brothers and sisters, something I didn't always relish due to the pressures heaped on me.

Before long, both on the school grounds as well as away from school, I found out that while Los Ranchos was a self-contained geographic area, within it were smaller cliques with names like "Dry Fish" and "Ranchitos." Unbeknownst to me—and I learned very quickly—each self-proclaimed territory boasted a gang. This was something new to me.

These avowed gangs, *gavillas*, consisted primarily of boys yet some girls belonged to the Ranchitos' clan. Both genders sported a dot tattooed on their right cheekbone. Their rivals showed off a tattoo as well but at the upper part of their nose bridge between the eyes. As if to convey toughness or evoke self-pity, they had the words HARD LUCK (in capital letters) tattooed on the fingers of their right and left hands, respectively, facing the onlooker. The Ranchitos group on the other hand, had LOVE tattooed on the fingers of their left hand to convey a more compassionate message. The rivalry between the two factions became patently obvious on the school grounds. Each one staked out their territory particularly while we were on recess. But jeering in whatever fashion was subtle since the teachers, not to mention the principal himself who walked and comingled with students, kept matters under control. Students dared not to be disruptive.

The reverse was unmistakable once the groups left school. Taunting and hollering at each other at times escalated to shoving matches or fisticuffs. Some gang members even took off their belts and wrapped them around their fists to deliver their blows. Following a long weekend, a member or two from either gang came to school on Monday morning with a bruised cheek if not a black or a puffed eye.

The ideal place for scuffles transpired at community dances held away from Dry Fish or Ranchitos, for example, the Alameda Community Center north of Los Ranchos. Once inside the dance hall, one group stood at one end of the hall or vice versa. In some cases, a boy from one rival gang would ask a girl from the opposite group to dance that potentially could result in sheer bedlam and thus end the dance right then and there.

For those of us who didn't wish to align ourselves with either group but instead remain neutral, the onus was on us. From time to time we were coaxed—or threatened—to join one of the gangs. If we declined, harassment of sorts oftentimes ensued. Somehow we, the nonconformists, prevailed by ostensibly banding together though not in a demonstrative way prone to antagonize one gang or the other.

Moreover, if you made friends with a classmate who was not Hispanic you ran the risk of being called a *lambe*, or apple polisher (aka, ass kisser) or other more ugly names. So being new to Los Ranchos I tried to walk a fine line and not make enemies.

I continued my treks home to join Mom for lunch unless the winter days were unbearably cold. One spring day, time eluded me, and I had to scurry back to school. In order not to be late, I took a shortcut through an empty lot near the ditch to our house. When I practically reached the other end of the property, I spotted two boys and a man. I had heard of the Lovato (not the real name) boys who had a reputation for being mean-spirited and troublemakers. Thinking that it was too late to turn around, I continued walking, which turned out to be a huge mistake. As I was about to cross the ditch one of the boys who was chopping weeds hollered at me, "¡Óyele! ¿Qué no sabes que esta propiedá no es pa tropellar?" (Listen here! Don't you know this property is not for you to trample over?) I smelled a rat so I only shrugged my shoulders. "¿Qué te cortó el gato la lengua?" (Did the cat eat your tongue?), asked the younger boy. Suddenly, I heard a voice behind me. "Hey, Tony. It's okay, man.

He's my new *vecino*, neighbor. He didn't mean no harm." I turned around. It was Art Harrison who lived next door to me. He came to my rescue. Thereafter he and I became the best of friends. Seventy years later, we're still friends.

Per chance I met a kid in my class named Jimmy Ketchum whose mother was in charge of the cafeteria where kids paid for a hot lunch. He asked if I would be interested in washing dishes at lunchtime in exchange for a hot meal. I talked to Mrs. Ketchum, followed by a conversation with Mom, who gave me permission to earn my lunch.

Pearl diving, a euphemism for dish washing, was hard and sweaty work. An additional drawback was not being able to eat lunch with Mom and play gin rummy. But in spite of these drawbacks, I earned my hot lunches until the end of the school year. That was an invaluable experience. It prepared me for an unexpected paying summer job ahead of beginning eighth grade at Garfield Junior High School.

Thanks to a couple of boys whom I befriended on the at Los Ranchos Elementary School, I learned of their summer jobs with the Matsubaras, a Japanese American family. They owned and operated a vegetable and fruit market on Fourth Street not far from the school. I inquired and was offered a job. My summer employment at the Matsubaras lasted three years, until I started high school in 1952.

The Matsubaras were a close-knit family. Besides the elderly father and mother, there were three sons. George was a manager at the Court Café on North Fourth Street in downtown Albuquerque and not directly affiliated with the family business. He did help his brother Frank on weekends. Frank the "kingmaker" managed the Matsubara Fruit and Vegetable Market. Charlie, on the other hand, was the workhorse who planted and harvested a variety of vegetables on their twenty-acre farm west of the Río Grande located south of the old Corrales Bridge. It was a family enterprise. That is how the Matsubaras earned their living.

A group of young boys, including me, spent the sweltering summer months working for Charlie at the farm. He had a gray 1939 van that he drove to transport us and his parents who helped with farm chores. Once there, we worked from eight o'clock in the morning until five in the evening, sometimes later if we wanted to earn extra money. The work, most of it on our knees or stooped over, was backbreaking. We hoed a variety of plants, thinned out others such as young carrots for them to grow bigger and better. Gathering potatoes after Charlie uprooted them with a contraption hooked to his tractor was hard work. Stooped over, we inched along, scooping up the potatoes from the soil and putting them in straw baskets or gunnysacks.

But the crop that we all loathed to pick was yellow onions. The actual work, though labor-intensive, just like harvesting potatoes, was not the problem. As the hot August sun beamed overhead, the stronger and more nauseous the onion smell; it stuck to your entire body with a vengeance. Mom even fixed an herbal concoction in a tin tub of warm water and made me bathe outdoors to lessen the smell as much as possible. The purported remedy was to no avail. I had to sleep in the open air on the bed of Dad's truck away from everyone else, above all my baby sister.

Equally as bad was the onion stench that saturated my clothes. Mom hated to wash them. Even after scrubbing them on a washboard in a tin tub of soap and water, two weeks later they still stunk to high heaven.

Above and beyond potatoes and onions, we helped Charlie harvest chile, carrots, cantaloupes, watermelons, radishes, and turnips. The crops were seasonal; that being the case, they were not all harvested at the same time. In addition, the Matsubaras had a tract of strawberries behind the family home on Fourth Street that helped augment the farm crops at the fruit market.

The summertime money I earned ranged from fifteen to twenty

dollars for forty-eight hours or more of work per week. There was no such thing as overtime pay or children's labor laws, but the job enabled me to buy clothing and other personal amenities that my father could not afford since he had a family of eight to feed—plus a sister and brother born later in Los Ranchos. What's more, with my Saturday paycheck I bought fruit and vegetables at a discount at the Matsubara Market to take home for the family to enjoy over the weekend. I especially liked buying a huge watermelon for everybody. Giving and sharing is something Mom taught us children. Being altruistic became second nature to me.

Aside from earning money, I learned to appreciate and respect Japanese culture and language. Thanks to the old folks who spoke no English, I became somewhat conversant in Japanese. Their struggle with a foreign language was a keen reminder of the problems I still wrestled with in English. Although I didn't realize it at the time, my curiosity about Japanese culture led to my avowed interest in Portuguese, Italian, and Latin. These are the languages I would one day study at the University of New Mexico besides refining my English and Spanish, my native tongue. (My military service in Germany and travels throughout Europe exposed me to different languages and cultures overall.)

As the summer came to an end, Charlie asked if I would like to help Frank at the family's fruit and vegetable market. Without hesitation I jumped at the opportunity. The transition from farmwork amounted to a promotion since my new job was cleaner and easier compared to hoeing, weeding, and harvesting crops. Another feature of my new job that I liked was carrying the customers' purchases to their cars. The women usually tipped me an occasional nickel or dime. Their gratuities were icing on the cake whereas the men tended to more frugal.

My summer job at the Matsubaras went smoothly. The same thing could be said about my first and only year—the seventh grade—at Los Ranchos School. Mrs. Meyerheim's class had been an enjoyable experience, thanks to her genuine devotion to her students. My interest in mathematics continued unabated. Social studies and art, though not of utmost interest to me, nevertheless added new dimensions to the overall pedagogical scheme of things.

My confidence in speaking and writing English improved little by little, but linguistic problems still nagged me as well as many of my Hispanic classmates. Having several monolingual English-speaking classmates was an undeniable asset. For example, whenever they wrote something on the blackboard that contained mistakes, the errors were visible to the entire class for Mrs. Meyerheim to correct. Some innocent blunders in mispronunciation of English words were humorous and added levity in class (e.g., shoes > *chews*), but we laughed together and not at one another. Mrs. Meyerheim guided us through our linguistic peaks and valleys. A sense of camaraderie and excitement prevailed in her class. I was to miss her and her class as well as some of my classmates.

I left Los Ranchos Elementary School amid mixed emotions prepared to begin the eighth grade at Garfield Junior High School.

Garfield Junior High— A Brand-New School

Garfield Junior High was a new school located on the 3500 block of North Sixth Street. (School kids thought of it as being on Fourth Street across from Saint Therese Church.) The school opened its doors in 1950–1951 to students from suburban neighborhoods, namely, Los Candelarias, Los Griegos, Los Duranes, as well as for those students like me from Los Ranchos de Alburquerque and Alameda in the North Valley.

Unlike Los Ranchos Elementary School where I walked to and

from school, I rode a school bus to Garfield School. This was my first experience riding a bus. It gave me a sense of independence and responsibility. In the morning the bus stopped at Los Ranchos Road and Second Street close to my house to pick me up and other kids from nearby homes. The bus driver made intermittent stops before we reached the school. Most of the kids on the bus were Hispanics, but a few were Anglos or of Japanese and Italian descent.

One new and redeeming factor at the junior high level was being exposed to more than one teacher who taught his or her own subject and areas of specialization. Whether they taught social studies, math, Spanish, business or English the teachers were for the most part exciting. I soon realized that a varied schedule at Garfield for some students was eminently better and even more conducive to learning than just having one uninspiring teacher all day long. Other students thought multiple classes lacked cohesion, were impersonal, and did not readily encourage a favorable rapport between teacher and pupils. To them it was akin to puddle jumping since the total pieces didn't add up to a complete whole.

In the course of the school year I had one or two teachers who were inspiring. One was Mr. Valerio who taught Spanish. He was hardly flamboyant, but he was devoted to his students and his subject. His class was important to me because for the first time in Albuquerque I could speak my native language in a classroom setting. Secondly, his emphasis on language and culture instilled pride regarding one's ethnicity and family roots. This aura of self-satisfaction was of paramount significance to me.

The least desirable of my teachers was a gentleman who taught woodshop. Boys viewed as troublemakers or disinterested in school were steered into his class (girls were advised to take home economics). It was not an ideal situation either for him or the students. The tense and seemingly unpleasant atmosphere engendered little learning.

To make matters worse, the first-year principal at Garfield Junior High who rode a motor scooter, perhaps an Italian Vespa, did not endear himself to students either. He was a disciplinarian with a no-nonsense attitude. Scores of students disliked his actions and nicknamed him Mr. Nutts because they thought he was crazy. The unflattering name prompted whispers and giggling among the student body, but he remained steadfast in his principles. He exemplified respect, fear, and ruthlessness.

A group of boys for whatever reason deflated the tires of a teacher's car. The principal did not take kindly to their prank. A shy and chubby kid, the perfect candidate due to his physical stature, was made the scapegoat. As punishment the principal made him run alongside his scooter—with only a few intermittent stops—from the school to Fourth Street and back again, four blocks total. He did this before classes in full view of students including those of us on the school bus as we arrived on the campus. The principal's reprimand reverberated through the school.

Students from nearby Los Duranes, Los Griegos, and Los Candelarias viewed the educational system as skewed toward inner-city kids. For them it was a matter of sink or swim. Oftentimes they became discouraged and quit school. As for semi-rural students from Los Ranchos and Alameda in the North Valley, they echoed the same feelings.

Lackluster teachers could be blamed and students, too, who were casual if not indifferent toward education. Many, including a number of my classmates, were just as culpable. They perceived the educational system as humdrum and for that reason rebelled against it.

I myself was not a good student. I lacked good studying skills, tips or strategies to prepare for and take tests as well as ways on how best to maximize my studying time. As a result, I felt as though I were constantly trying to play catch up. My struggles with English still haunted me.

Toward the end of the school year I, like countless other students, was glad to leave Garfield Junior High. I did so with a tad of ambivalence. At best it became patently clear that one teacher can indeed make a difference in motivating you toward achieving undreamed-of educational goals (for more on this topic see chapter 5).

Washington Junior High—A Total Blur

Just when I thought the challenges of getting an education could not get worse, they did. My school days at Washington Junior High (1951–1952), located on South Tenth Street in Albuquerque, remain a veritable blur to this day. An unpleasant atmosphere, I regret to say, prevailed in and outside the classroom. Rivalries among gangs that did not exist at Garfield Junior High emerged and worsened as tensions rose between them. Cliques from Los Ranchos and Alameda now found themselves confronted by inner-city factions from Old Town (Sawmill) and Barelas, south of downtown Albuquerque. New antagonists—at least from my perspective—were the pseudo cowboys (mostly Anglos with one or two Hispanics) who wore boots, Levi's, and large metal belt buckles.

To make matters worse, a number of Hispanic gang members brought to school a variety of weapons—on the sly, of course. Among them were pocket knives, chains, and brass knuckles. One kid named Tacho even carried a short machete under his shirt. For those of us who were not allied with any particular group, the arsenal of weapons was frightening since we could inadvertently get caught in the middle of a confrontation.

Baffling, too, was the repertoire of inner-city gobbledygook that the cool or crazy *vatos*, or dudes, employed. Their speech was akin to code words and incomprehensible to most of us. Here in random order are some examples: *trola* (match), *grifo* (pothead), *refinar* (to eat), *calcos* (shoes), *chante* (home), *ramfla* (car), *lana* (money), *yesca* (pot or marijuana), *entabicar* (to lock up in jail), *garras* (clothes), *escamar* (to scare), and *tacuche* (suit). These esoteric or subcultural terms are what many students like me and my Los Ranchos compatriots learned outside the classroom.

Monday morning for teachers as well as students was the most eerie day of the week. Violent clashes over the weekend between inner-city gang members at local barrio dances were common. I recall to this day one Monday morning the empty desk behind me. My classmate with the surname García was stabbed to death over the weekend by a rival gang member. On other occasions, gang members showed up with black eyes or puffed-up cheeks after getting pummeled. Girls who belonged to one gang or the other did not escape from being roughed up either. One couldn't help but to feel sorry for the teachers, most of whom tried their best to teach under an unsettling environment and trying circumstances.

On weekends I continued to work at the Matsubaras Fruit and Vegetable Market, which kept me occupied and out of trouble. I did endure periodic teasing at school from my peers. Their playfulness stemmed from jealousy because I was earning money, and they weren't. On the other hand, I, like other students who did not belong to any particular group, still had to endure taunting or harassment from gang members. Constant fear hovered over many of us at Washington Junior High. It was hardly conducive to learning.

Closer to home, the person I feared the most was my father. He was strict through and through. One given weekend a small group of us teenagers from Los Ranchos attended a dance in Bernalillo where I was born. A fellow probably nineteen years old or younger whom I knew from Los Ranchos came up to me where I was sitting. "Hey, *compa*, would you watch this knife [a stiletto] for me while I dance?" he asked courteously. "Sure, why not," I responded innocently.

Shortly thereafter the sheriff and his deputies arrived unannounced at the dance hall. A commotion ensued and everyone scurried and headed for the exit door, but the sheriff and a deputy blocked the entrance and did not allow anyone to leave. Apparently the sheriff had been alerted about a potential brawl between rival gangs from Bernalillo and Albuquerque's North Valley. The other officers began frisking the boys on the dance floor as well as those like me who were sitting down. Quickly I sat on the knife to disguise it. "Stand up!" commanded a deputy. All at once, the knife hit the floor for him to see.

Because of allegedly carrying a weapon, I was booked at the Sandoval County jail in Bernalillo along with a fellow older than me from Alameda whom I knew. The deputy herded both of us into the backseat of his car. I was scared to death. The first person I thought of was my dear mother. She would be heartbroken. As for my father, he would be livid.

Somehow my parents were notified of my misstep. My father predictably was furious. "If his sentence is three months, double it!" Luckily my step-grandfather in Bernalillo who had a certain political clout bailed me out. My mother was relieved, but my father didn't speak to me for several months. His aloofness was more mortifying than the filthy, rat-infested, and squalid conditions of the jail cell where I spent one unforgettable night. The experience had a sobering effect on my young life. I vowed to be a good son if not a better student.

As always, learning for a kid like me from the hinterland continued both inside and outside the classroom. Turmoil and fights at Washington Junior High School, or nearby Robinson Park at lunchtime between rival gangs, remain embedded in my psyche. The incidents constitute a regrettable part of my public education.

Lackadaisical teachers did not help matters either. To this day

I can't remember the name of a single teacher at Washington Junior High, and it isn't because the unfortunate souls weren't trying to discharge their responsibilities. On the contrary, the majority of students were both the culprits and detractors. The social pressures on the student body overall were overbearing, but many students, unfazed by all the distractions, remained loyal to their studies. Others no doubt longed to leave Washington Junior High School, yours truly among them. For me the entire school year to this day remains a veritable blur.

Albuquerque High School, a step higher in the educational hierarchy, I surmised could only be better. A new school, new administrators, new teachers, and new students were ample reasons to be optimistic. I cautiously looked forward to a new experience with a modicum of excitement and anticipation.

Turning Over a New Leaf

THE GLOOMY DAYS AT WASHINGTON Junior High were behind me. A new beginning dawned as I prepared for Albuquerque High School, the standard bearer and the larger of the two city high schools in the 1950s. (Highland High School was the other one.) Albuquerque High was located at Central Avenue (Route 66) and Broadway.

The self-contained campus formed a rectangular layout with a large courtyard and a statue of the bulldog mascot prominently situated in the center of Bulldog Plaza. The dark brown buildings that sported gray trimmings and large windows added to the school's stark appearance. All the same, a sense of comfort and solitude greeted and enveloped students upon entering the campus, insulating you from the hustle and bustle of the outside world. I was eager to embark on a new educational venture.

The school bus ride from Los Ranchos was no longer new per se, but the route to Albuquerque High School was shorter and less circuitous than the one to Washington Junior High School. The student ridership from the North Valley, that is to say, Alameda and Los Ranchos, remained essentially unchanged.

Gradually I began to get acclimated to the new school: its environs, teachers, and administrators. Aside from dedicated teachers and friendly staff, there is one individual who stood out among them—Glen O. Ream. He was the principal my sophomore and junior years at Albuquerque High (1952–1954) and had served in that position for more than twenty-five years. Neatly dressed, he and his bowtie were inseparable. Mr. Ream was not only a veritable gentleman but a true friend of the students. He was visible on campus, visiting and chatting with students at all times, plus he invariably inquired how you were doing in your studies. He exemplified the consummate administrator whose empathy with students was unequivocal. Mr. Ream too eased whatever tensions surfaced between rival groups.

Once I enrolled in my classes what piqued my interest was the mixture of students. Some came from inner-city neighborhoods such as upscale Huning Heights; others hailed from San José, an impoverished district.

Hispanic gangs analogous to those at Washington Junior High were not as visible. More noticeable were the so-called cowboys, but their presence was more symbolic than outright hostile against Hispanic rival factions. Several Hispanos who joined the cowboy clan wore pearl button shirts, wide leather belts with huge metal buckles, and wrangler boots, only to be sneered at by their own compatriots. These crossover types were in a no-win situation. Whenever members from opposing groups appeared in the same classroom, serious and courageous teachers kept matters under control.

A few teachers enjoyed a better reputation than others, which is understandable, whereas others stood out for different reasons. One teacher who commanded a lot of attention was Dr. Eldred Harrington who taught chemistry. He was deemed a genius as well as being renowned for stinking up the campus. On days when the smell of rotten eggs emerged from his laboratory in the southeast corner of the school, the pronouncements were indisputable. "It's Dr. Harrington and his students at work in his chemistry laboratory." But the stereotypical looks of a genius—at least in the eyes of most students—were unmistakable. His unruly curly hair and a bowtie were his trademark. Plus, he had a droopy right eye. Students who enrolled in Dr. Harrington's class either had an appreciable interest in chemistry or they found him intriguing.

Of the various teachers I studied under during my two-year stint at Albuquerque High, I have both fond and mixed memories. The pervasive social malaise that plagued the school—at least from my vantage point—and uninspiring teachers linger to this day. My interest in the Spanish language and culture from my days at Garfield Junior High was rekindled thanks to Mrs. Ann Komadina. She not only was inspiring but someone who showed concern for students' academic performance and improvement.

Other teachers' names come to mind but for different or less desirable reasons. My English teacher, Mr. Ellen Williams, was a no-nonsense teacher whose command of his subject was undeniable if you cared to learn, but he, too, was reputed as being aloof from students. An additional flaw—and he was not unique in this respect—was treating his students as though they were a homogenous group irrespective of their cultural backgrounds. Students from diverse socioeconomic or ethnic backgrounds did not expect special treatment. But they anticipated a more humane and universal understanding of the linguistic problems that they brought from home. Mr. Williams, like some of his colleagues, consciously or not oftentimes overlooked or was indifferent toward students' cultural backgrounds.

There were added challenges, of course, in particular for students from rural or semi-rural areas who lacked the preparation for certain courses. Biology is a case in point. At the behest of my counselor, Mr. Robert Ivey, I enrolled in his biology class. The plants, animals, and birds indigenous to New Mexico were not as alien to me as those species found beyond our borders featured in our textbook.

Some of us were introduced for the first time to the intricacies of life cycles, reproductive systems, cell membranes, and fungi ("there's fungus among us," became a classroom joke). The climax or low point in biology for me was the anatomizing of frogs in the laboratory that most students either found hilarious or repulsive. Except for the butchering of animals (e.g., La Matanza) in the open air at my grandparents' ranch where I spent my boyhood, dissecting frogs was far removed from anything I had experienced or witnessed heretofore. That was true as well for other students who came from rural New Mexico.

In the same building where I studied biology, I had a typing class with Mrs. Jean Marsh. She, like my English teacher, was strict, perhaps unduly. One of her techniques or approaches was to cover the keyboards of the Underwood typewriters with dishtowels or white cloths. As we practiced over and over again those unforgettable and ubiquitous words, "Now is the time for all good men to come to the aid of their country," Mrs. Marsh had the uncanny ability to sneak up behind you and smack your knuckles with a long wooden stick if you dared to peek at the keyboard. Aside from her unorthodox and harsh treatment (students nicknamed her Harsh Mrs. Marsh), I, for one, learned how to type. Of the entire array of subjects that I enrolled for in high school, typing doubtless has proven to be one of the most beneficial in my public education experience.

As my education at Albuquerque High School progressed, Spanish, my native language, which was spoken at home, became one of my favorite subjects. I could easily relate to the linguistic and cultural trappings I had been immersed in since childhood, unencumbered by the difficulties I faced with English, my adopted language.

Not forgotten was my interest in mathematics that waned in the intervening years since I left Los Ranchos Elementary School. At Albuquerque High School I studied algebra with Mrs. Clara Barnhart and geometry with a young teacher named Jerry Davis. I fared all right in algebra even though I found terms such as variables, constants, and exponents, difficult to comprehend. They clashed dramatically with common terms such as equals ($=$), times ($\times$), and pluses ($+$) that I understood well. Plane geometry's application of figures (i.e., shapes, lines, circles, etc.) in Mr. Davis' class defied my comprehension. The young teacher's lack of pedagogical expertise did not help matters, either. In the final analysis, I lost interest in mathematics.

Aside from electives, we were required to fulfill a specified number of credit hours in science, social science, math, English, and physical education in order to graduate. Physical education (PE) was presumed to be fun and games. Baseball and track and field were outdoor sports; basketball and volleyball were played in the school's gymnasium. Sad but true, one of the least memorable moments in the range of PE classes is swimming.

Since the school did not have a pool, for swimming lessons the coach led his students to the YMCA (often referred to as the Y) located on First Street and Central Avenue in downtown Albuquerque. Our instructor was a short, stocky man with dark, hairy eyebrows and wiry hair who had the indisputable reputation of being a disciplinarian as well as meanspirited. I had been raised in the desert and because of that was eager to learn how to swim, but those hopes were dashed in short order. Once inside the YMCA, the coach lined us up on one side of the pool, starting from the deep end with large blue letters EIGHT–TEN feet painted on both sides of the pool underneath the water.

Alas I ended up at the deep end of the pool. Then I heard the coach shout, "On the count of three, jump in!" As his words echoed in the cavernous pool I hollered, "Coach, I can't swim!" "That's why you're here," he responded rather coldly. "Ready?" He howled though this time his words seemed to bounce off the brick walls. "But coach," I screamed, this time in utter panic. "I can't swim!" At that moment he walked to where I standing. He counted aloud from one to three and he pushed me into the water. I swatted uncontrollably. As I gasped for air and spitted water, I faintly heard one of the students. "Coach, coach, he's drowning! He's drowning!" A few seconds later I miraculously surfaced from under water. Suddenly the words "Hold on! Hold on!" rang out. I saw a wooden pole, grabbed it, and hung on for dear life until the coach pulled me out of the water. I was stunned and shaking. "Are you okay?" A boy nearby asked. I shook my head yes. "You're white as a bedsheet," he added. The coach, true to form, never inquired of my well-being. His name shall remain anonymous.

The antithesis in temperament was the other PE coach, Pete McDavid. He was strict but friendly. Years later (the 1960s), he distinguished himself as athletic director at the University of New Mexico. At that point, I took time off from my studies and used my Student Activity Card to attend track meets at Zimmerman Field across from Zimmerman Library. I saw super athletes compete such as Adolph Plummer who broke the record in the 440-yard dash, and the Olympian Dick Howard whose specialty was the 440-yard hurdles. Plus, I saw Don Perkins play football before he became a running back for the Dallas Cowboys.

Learning time and again occurred away from the classroom. A fortuitous thing happened while I was at Albuquerque High. I got a new job at Zía Gardens Market thanks to my next-door neighbor, Art (Arturo) Harrison, who worked there as a cashier. He asked if I would be interested in working with him. Of course I said yes mindful that to return to the Matsubaras' farm to hoe, weed, and harvest crops was not a pleasant thought.

Art talked to Joe Pacheco the owner of Zía Gardens at 6818 North Second Street situated about a mile from my house. He offered me a job sacking groceries and carrying them to customers' vehicles. What's more, I helped stock food shelves, and thereafter I learned to take care of the vegetable bins. Of course sweeping and mopping floors became part of my duties. With part of the money I earned I bought lunch at high school. That way Mom didn't have to pack me a daily sack lunch. I was forever thankful to Art Harrison with whom I have remained friends since we first met in 1949 when my family moved to Los Ranchos de Alburquerque. I worked at Zía Gardens Market from 1952 until 1955.

Following two years at Albuquerque High School (1952–1954),

I, like countless North Valley students, had a choice either to remain at AHS or to transfer to Valley High School. Valley, as it came to be known, was a brand-new school in Los Candelarias, northwest of downtown Albuquerque. Students from nearby Los Griegos, Los Candelarias, and Los Duranes plus outlying areas such as Alameda and Los Ranchos opted for Valley High School because it was closer to their homes.

My senior year (1954–1955) proved to be the most rewarding and exciting of my public education. Self-fulfillment was due to new and caring teachers, some of whom had taught at Albuquerque High School the previous year. They, too, seemed invigorated to be at a new school.

I recall those teachers fondly but more for their avowed devotion to teaching and rapport with students than my interest in the subjects. Among those educators were Marie Hayes, physical education; JP Bygel, bookkeeping and typing; Clinton F. Hurley, English; Ed DiNello, science; Robert Lalicker, history, and Ernest Stapleton, counselor and history.

I cherished being part of the groundbreaking class of 1955 that consisted about 115 graduating seniors. A multiplicity of responsibilities fell on our shoulders: choosing the school colors (maroon, gray, and gold); selecting the mascot, the Viking; naming our yearbook, the Saga; and, picking the school song, "My Friend Cherry Pink and Apple Blossom White." What's more, we chose our class colors, orchid and white, as well as the class motto, "We lead— others follow." We made epic decisions that nowadays, sixty-plus years later, constitute part of the school's enduring legacy.

On a lesser scale, but important to me, was having belonged to several clubs. Among them were the Hi-Y Club, an extension of YMCA responsible for providing service to the school and community, and the Hot Rod Club known as the Rambling Rods.

My interest in cars, as was true of those like Ron López and his brother Richard, Don Pruitt, Bob Geisler, and Frank Keller, all of whom belonged to the club, was "to improve hot rods and to customize automobiles." Don Pruitt had a hot rod (photo appears in Saga yearbook). He fulfilled in part our mission under Mr. Henry Shrieber, the club's sponsor.

Our pastime with regard to cars evolved from the aura of automobiles with dual or loud mufflers, half-moon headlights, windshield sun visors, and low rear ends, the predecessors of today's endearing lowriders. There was a drawback. Police thought of those with modified cars as rebels and a menace on city streets, but it was more of a stereotype and misplaced perception by law officers.

My employment at Zía Gardens Market enabled me to buy—with Dad's consent—a 1950 Chevrolet. I paid approximately $1,600, a lot of money in those days. Buying a car proved to be a bittersweet experience. Car payments in addition to gas, oil, and other personal incidentals consumed virtually every penny that I earned. There were times when I didn't have enough money to replace my socks with holes in them.

Many of my classmates envied me for having a car, but little did they know that what lurked behind a nice car was a penniless billfold. It was horrible, but I did pay for the car on a time-honored fashion before I graduated from high school.

Prior to joining the army I sold the car for $550 to the brother of a good friend of mine at Valley High School. My monetary losses due to depreciation made owning a car for the first time painful. In future years I learned to be more judicious on how I spent my money.

But for me it was vitally important to look at the positive experience at Valley High School. Camaraderie among virtually every senior was phenomenal. No one was ignored unless you chose not to be part of the fanfare throughout the year—and there were a few schoolmates, the shy ones, who chose not to participate in the school's senior activities.

A highlight of the school year was the senior prom. One of our classmates was escorted by Al Sánchez. Later dubbed Al "Hurricane," he was destined to become a legend and mainstay in the annals of music in our beloved New Mexico, the Land of Enchantment.

The feeling of togetherness at Valley High School was unambiguous. It was a milestone year for seniors and future graduating classes based on our groundbreaking initiatives and undertakings. One fellow graduate and a close friend who was a mover and shaker in organizing class reunions over the years to honor our graduating class was Barbara Faris (Ruther). (She passed away in Santa Fe November 2022.) Her husband Jerry has become a dear friend as well.

I should add, lest I'd be remiss (by no means an afterthought) but one of our steadfast supporters was our beloved Ernest "Ernie" Stapleton. He served as counselor and advisor to students and was "never too busy with individual student problems to help plan a party or sponsor a dance to encourage school spirit" (Saga 1955). He maintained this esprit de corps throughout his educational career and thereafter by attending our school reunions. He passed on April 12, 2016. He was eighty-nine years old.

Administrators and faculty joined hands and never failed to put students' needs at the forefront. From the principal, Captain Warren Smart, a transplant from Albuquerque High School, including those teachers mentioned earlier, to our benevolent counselor Ernest Stapleton, they singularly and collectively were the bedrock that led to unforgettable moments at Valley High School.

I was not a very good student, but I managed to squeeze by with passing grades to graduate. That momentous occasion occurred on Wednesday, May 25, 1955, at Valley High School's gymnasium. The venerable Mr. John Milne delivered the introduction. He was superintendent of schools and a stalwart in the Albuquerque School System for more than forty years. It was a memorable night for me and my parents: my mother who never went to school, basked in the excitement. My father, who quit school in the fifth grade to help his parents on the farm, rejoiced as I received my diploma.

For me to graduate from high school was an enormous accomplishment given the trials and tribulations incurred in the public school system, but what loomed in the future was nebulous at best. Young and immature I did not have a clear vision what to do with my life. Most classmates faced the same dilemma. Getting a job was uppermost in everyone's mind. Hardly anyone I knew spoke of going to college, earning a degree, and embarking on a professional career.

After graduation I worked full-time the entire summer at Zía Gardens Market until I joined the US Army in the fall. I truly enjoyed stocking shelves and tending to the vegetable and fruit bins. On occasion, I even learned from Joe Pacheco, the owner, how to grind hamburger meat and do other simple chores in the butcher shop. In addition, I had gotten promoted to cashier. This enabled me, among other things, to appreciate how meticulous housewives were—the main shoppers back then—by taking advantage of weekly specials and sales.

Most of all, I delighted in meeting customers from Nara Visa, the local neighborhood, as well as Pueblo Indians (Native Americans) from Sandía, Santa Ana, and San Felipe who stopped daily to purchase a few staples on their way home from work. But the bulk of their grocery shopping came every two weeks—the 1st and 15th of each month. On these days Joe Pacheco ordered a large supply of lamb—above all legs of lamb that the Pueblo Indians loved. Whenever it appeared as though he would run out of lamb, I drove Joe's white 1952 Oldsmobile to Schwartzman's Meat Packing Company in Albuquerque's South Valley. My contact person there was Colombo, a jovial Italian whom I liked—and he liked me. There I picked up the lamb and other meats.

Other times if we ran out of certain grocery items, I drove to Charles Ilfeld on North First Street in downtown Albuquerque to pick up the merchandise. Regrettably, these trips decreased as Joe Pacheco, for reasons unknown to me, couldn't afford to replenish the merchandise we sold. The shelves became increasingly bare, and sadness and depression hit me more and more. Loyal customers came in the store but left equally distressed because we didn't have the groceries they needed, not even household staples.

Joe Pacheco as it turned out was on the cusp of going broke. But throughout this sad ordeal, I remained loyal to him till the bitter end. He was a wonderful and trusted boss.

I managed to get my job back with the new owners, but they were a far cry from Joe Pacheco both in management style and temperament. Dressed in suit and tie, they were stoic, aloof, and too business-like for my taste. I missed Joe's humming and singing while he cut sides of beef and pork chops to sell over the counter. I missed Joyful Joe.

By September I received a formal letter from the recruiting office in downtown Albuquerque to report for induction into the US Army. Two other Valley High classmates, Gabriel García (no relation) and Alfonso Gurulé, received similar letters. We had volunteered for the draft—a two-year assignment rather than three years if you enlisted—soon after we graduated from high school. We remained together the duration of our tour of military duty, 1955–1957, while we were stationed at Ft. Knox, Kentucky, and Hanau, Germany.

At Zía Gardens Market I said goodbye to Joe Pacheco's brother-in-law Mackey, a good friend of mine who now worked for the new owners, and to several of my favorite customers. Among them were Mrs. Barnett,* Frank Faris (Barbara Faris [Ruther] was his niece), Mrs. Greer, Joe Solís's family, including the daughter Charlotte,

---

* While I was stationed at Ft. Hanau, Germany, she mailed me a box of home-baked bizcochitos, but they were all crumbled to smithereens. I ate them just the same.

Mrs. Corley, and Mrs. Crossman, co-owner of the Last Stop Bar and Liquor Store on Second Street and Osuna.

Another business couple who shopped at Zía Gardens Market was Mrs. Brown who along with her husband owned La Placita Restaurant in Old Town. Last but not least was my dear friend Sadie Koury. Her modest but efficient cafe next to the Crossmans' business was renowned for her hamburgers and hearty breakfasts served to the early morning workers (e.g., construction). Overtime I must have delivered hundreds of pounds of hamburger meat to Sadie's little restaurant. (At present the building is a tire repair shop.) Today her youngest sister, Betty Jo and her family are the proud owners of restaurants that bare Sadie's name. (Sadie passed away in 1986 when I lived in Colorado.)

Bagging groceries and carrying them out to my favorite customers is firmly rooted in my bank of pleasant remembrances. I'm indebted to Art Harrison for the job at Zía Gardens Market (the building at 6818 on Second Street still stands) and to Joe Pacheco the owner. During my days at Zía Gardens I learned about work ethics, about managing one's finances and, most importantly, about getting along with people.

I was inculcated with these invaluable qualities at home—thanks to my beloved parents—that served me well in my senior year at Valley High School and later throughout my educational career after I was discharged from the army in 1957.

Time, Perseverance, and Encouragement

IN LATE SUMMER OF 1957, a group of freshmen and I stood in line on a sultry day to consult with our academic advisor at the University of New Mexico (UNM) where the duck pond stands today. Though strangers onto one another an infrequent chatter or giggle punctuated the silence among one of the boys or girls. Perspiration dripped from my brow as the scorching sun beamed mercilessly on us. I could see my face reflected on my shined black shoes as I glanced at the desert-colored dirt. Step by step I and the other prospective students inched along like listless worms.

I was discharged from the US Army in late June. For me standing in line to fetch a meal at the Mess Hall or to purchase a ticket at the movie theater was still fresh in my mind. Waiting is something I got accustomed to in my two-year stint both at Ft. Knox, Kentucky, and in Hanau, Germany. The ubiquitous military adage of "hurry up and wait" for the moment seemed apropos even at a university.

While I waited my turn, I contemplated what had brought me to this stage in my young life. Soon after my two Valley High School classmates and I were discharged from the army at Camp Chaffee, Arkansas, we embarked on our long journey to Albuquerque on a Greyhound bus. I came home to Los Ranchos de Alburquerque to get reacquainted with my parents and my seven siblings. With ample time on my hands as I adjusted to a new and unregimented way of life, I walked to Zía Gardens Market not far from my house to inquire about a job. As mentioned previously, I worked there as a cashier and stock boy prior to serving in the military. The supermarket under new owners and management did not have a job opening.

Leaving Zía Gardens Market I ran into Mrs. Mary Crossman (mentioned in the previous chapter) by sheer serendipity. I knew her from my high school days when on occasion, I delivered groceries to her as well as to Sadie, my friend who owned Sadie's Cafe next door. After exchanging pleasantries, she asked what I planned to do now that my tour in the army was over.

"My plans are to get a job and then go to college the spring semester," I responded.

"You will do no such thing!" she exclaimed in a motherly albeit friendly manner. "Once you have a job and start earning money, your plans to further your education will go by the wayside." I listened attentively. "I tell you what," she continued. "You remember Mr. Robert Lalicker your history teacher at Valley High School where you and Steve (her son and I were friends) attended, right? He is now an assistant to President Tom Popejoy at the University of New Mexico. I suggest you go see him about enrolling—and the sooner the better. And, oh yes, you tell Mr. Lalicker I sent you there."

I did not ponder her advice for long; it seemed sound and well-intentioned. I went to see Mr. Lalicker, renewed acquaintances, and then he apprised me of the bureaucratic process in applying for admission and registration.

After filling out an application, I had my high school academic transcript from Valley High School sent to the Office of Admissions. Soon thereafter I received a notice of eligibility, which included a registration number and instructions for registering. All freshmen were automatically enrolled in the University College for advisement and guidance to help them ultimately in deciding on a major course of study best suited for his or her interests. In addition, prior to registration freshmen were required to take a battery of scholastic aptitude examinations administered by the University Counseling and Testing Services. One of those tests included the English Proficiency Examination, which was destined to become one of my nemeses.

An assembly was held in Carlisle Gymnasium to welcome incoming freshmen. One of the administrators who greeted us was the director of testing services. His immediate words did not convey a warm reception. "I want each of you to look at the person to your left and the one to your right," he said in a gruffly and indifferent tone of voice, and heads moved in either direction. "Four years from now," he continued, "only one of you will be among those receiving a degree." Whether his unscientific prediction was valid or not, his words were hardly encouraging. His heartless remarks evoked murmuring of sorts. Later on, as I retook the English Proficiency Examination for the second time, I learned that the administrator in question enjoyed the unflattering sobriquet of Dr. Mean-Goat.

Following aptitude tests and orientation, student advisement was the pre-ultimate step before officially registering for semester courses. Because of my interest in business, given that I had worked in a supermarket for several years, I was to see a Dr. William J. Parish, professor of business, who had been assigned as my academic advisor. I was now a bona fide student in the University College for up to two years. In the interim I had to declare a major and henceforth transfer to an appropriate college (e.g., Arts and Sciences) and a major department.

I was about to meet with Dr. Parish after standing in the sweltering heat for what seemed like an eternity. I had observed the looks on the faces of students as they left his office. Some had a smile; others were glum or looked angry. "Where will I fall in the scale of glee, sadness or anger?" I asked myself. I would soon find out.

I opened the door to Dr. Parish's office located in World War II barracks. (I believe it was Yakota Hall.) I walked in. Sitting behind a large, imposing wooden desk was a bespectacled man with glasses halfway down the bridge of his nose. Without introducing himself he asked. "Are you Na, na, . . . Mr. García?" as he struggled to pronounce my first name. "Nasario," I interrupted, trying to be helpful. "Nasario García," I said pronouncing my entire name. "Please have a seat," he said, and I sat in this wide wooden chair that seemed to swallow my average frame.

I glanced at him as he wriggled in his wooden chair. He peered at some papers and then he leafed through them. I waited anxiously for the next words to spew from his mouth. His stern look did not impress me as that of a friendly person. Dr. Parish finally looked up and straight at me.

"Stand up for a moment," and he gestured with a pencil in his right hand. "You see these curved red lines?" Then he pointed to a sheet of white paper with black vertical and horizontal lines. "The red lines are the scores from your entrance examinations. Your scores are so far below the national average, I'll give you no more than one semester on this campus."

His callous words struck me like a solid blow to the gut. "Nevertheless," he continued, "let's draw up a class schedule for you. The normal load per semester is fifteen hours, but I strongly advise you to take only twelve hours," as he drove the dagger of humiliation deeper. After a brief discussion regarding what courses to enroll for, he approved my schedule. "There you are! That's your schedule for the semester. Come see me at mid-semester when I'll have your midterm grades. We'll see where you stand academically at that time."

There was nothing flamboyant about the schedule since certain courses were part of the core curriculum. Besides English and Speech, I signed up for Intermediate Algebra and Elementary Spanish.

I thanked Dr. Parish and left his office livid. I kicked the dirt and scuffed my polished shoes. The angry look on my face must have startled the girl next in line. "I'll show you, you bastard," I muttered under my breath. I was in no mood to accept his piercing and hurtful words at face value. My father had always taught me and my siblings never to accede to defeat without a good fight. His words "El que regaña a veces se ahoga con sus mismas palabras" (He who scolds you, oftentimes ends up choking on his own words) rang loud and clear. Time, the determiner of all things, together with persistence and good fortune, ultimately would tell the tale whether I succeeded or failed.

Notwithstanding the meager army salary of seventy to eighty-four dollars per month, I had managed to save a modest amount of money at the Albuquerque National Bank in downtown Albuquerque. This enabled me to devote fulltime to my studies during the first academic year, 1957–1958, without having to work. But alas, I never envisioned the multiplicity of unforeseen academic problems that awaited me because of being ill-prepared for the university. My poor command of English was among them. I soon learned that my reading, writing, and comprehension skills were inadequate for an incoming freshman. I felt like a wrestler with one arm tied behind his back. My two-year stint in the army had not helped my English one iota. I subsequently had to enroll for no credit in Remedial English, a euphemism for dumbbell English, which was personally and psychologically degrading.

To use the public school system as a scapegoat would have been expeditious, but after some soul-searching I shunned that notion. I was willing to assume responsibility for my educational shortcomings. I was not a good student in public schools, as mentioned earlier, but to be perfectly candid, I found most teachers—not all—a veritable bore and not very inspiring. As a consequence, I quietly rebelled against them and did only average work in the classroom. I was now suffering the consequences for my inclinations and misguided notions. "Whatever transpired in the past must be rectified in the present. The onus was on me," I thought to myself.

The semester was in full swing, and I was eager to begin my

studies. To minimize the cost of commuting daily sixteen miles round trip from my parents' home in Los Ranchos de Alburquerque to the university, I decided, at my father's behest, to stay at my paternal grandparents' home in Martíneztown. This is where my family and I lived in Grandma's storage room from 1945–1949 after we moved from the Río Puerco Valley. Every morning my father stopped on his way to work to drop off my lunch that Mom happily prepared for me. From Grandpa and Grandma's house to the campus in my 1951 Ford was a scant fifteen minutes.

With a tad of anxiety but eager, nonetheless, I departed early on Monday morning to attend my first day of classes. I secured a parking space in front of Zimmerman Library on Yale Blvd. My classes, English, Algebra, Spanish, and Speech, were in Mitchell Hall catty-corner from the library.

English, my first class, was on the second floor. I recall that vividly because of the instructor whose name was Mrs. Pigg. She was quick to emphasize that it was spelled with two *g*'s. Her course for a variety of reasons proved to be invaluable. A primary requirement was a research paper. For whatever inexplicable reason, I chose the unlikely topic of "The Tennessee Valley Authority." To help her students in research methodology Mrs. Pigg of her own volition took the time to acquaint us with the physical layout of Zimmerman Library. We were briefed on how to use the card catalog (nowadays all library holdings are accessible on computers), the numbering system (i.e., Dewey Decimal System, today maintained by the Online Computer Library Center [OCLC]), and other helpful research pointers.

Consulting and ferreting out information from scholarly journals and books, combined with jotting notes on three-by-five cards, remains one of the most worthwhile experiences of my undergraduate studies. What's more, Mrs. Pigg cautioned us concerning the proper use of footnotes, citing accurately primary and secondary sources, as well as the seriousness of plagiarism.

Above and beyond the research paper, *The Odyssey* by Homer was required reading. This esoteric classic was the first novel I ever read in my life. Yet because of my childhood exposure to the tenets of folklore in rural New Mexico I could relate to the phantasma-gorical Cyclops and the third eye. To a certain extent they were reminiscent of the strange and at times bizarre stories I heard as a young boy: mysterious bouncing balls of fire that chased humans at dusk; La Mamona, the bull snake that sucked dry a cow's udder; or the colorful yellow and green lizards whose acid-like spittle that could eat away at your skin. These Homeric-type images somewhat alleviated my problems with English.

The course I recall rather humorously if not intriguing is Speech for Foreign Language Students. Every freshman was required to take a speech test. If a student showed any defects in speaking, he or she either had to enroll in the abovementioned course or take Speech Improvement (remedial speech) to rectify whatever speech prob-lems were determined by the professor in charge. The professor who tested me was Dr. St. Onge.

"García is the name. Is that correct?" he asked employing only my last name. I had a feeling he was intimidated by the name Na-sario. "Yes, that's me," I responded, at which point he handed me a sheet of paper. "I want you to read the first few lines," he said as I walked up to the podium in front of the classroom. I read from the prepared passage while the rest of the students waited their turn. "Okay, that's enough. Where are you from?" the professor asked. "I'm from here, Albuquerque." "But where did you get 'gotta do dat' and some of the other strange pronunciations?" He exhibited a puzzled look on his face. "Sir, I guess it's because of my army buddies. One was an Italian from Waterbury, Connecticut, or my Irish friends from Queens, New York. My best friend Terry Murphy was from Cleveland."

"Given your linguistic idiosyncrasies," he added as though I comprehended the meaning of this last word, "I suggest you take Speech 3—Speech for Foreign Language Students." The course, taught by Dr. St. Onge himself, was designed primarily for students who spoke English with a foreign accent as well as those who lacked oral fluency. To be a native New Mexican and treated as a foreign student was certainly a surprise. On the other hand, I also found it ironic given the fact that my family roots transcend several centuries in New Mexico. Plus, English is considered a foreign language in our state. In the final analysis, I enjoyed the fine points of speech in Dr. St. Onge's course that proved to be rather serendipitous and helpful.

I enrolled in Fundamentals of Speech, which prepared you in the delivery of original and extemporaneous speeches. Dr. Chreist, a gregarious gentleman and a good teacher, taught the course. His course and that of Dr. St. Onge served me well later in my academic career as a university professor. I learned to apply the mechanics of public speaking that were helpful in becoming an effective and successful teacher in the classroom.

As the semester progressed living at my grandparents' home without indoor facilities became an inconvenience. Besides, I felt sorry for Mom who insisted on preparing my daily lunches that Dad brought me every morning. I looked upon both kind gestures as a burden on my parents.

So, without hurting anyone's feelings, I decided to rent a private room from a Mrs. Ernest close to the university. The third-floor room with a communal bathroom (no shower) for twenty dollars per month was a vast improvement over my grandparents' accommodations. Her Victorian-style home was located at 1901 Silver SE, two blocks directly south of Hodgin Hall, the cornerstone of the university. The room with a queen-size bed, a small writing desk, and a modest-size walk-in closet was to be my home from 1957–1962. During that time Mrs. Ernest, who hailed from Coffeyville, Kansas, and I became good friends. In five years she only raised the rent by five dollars per month.

For meals I made arrangements to eat breakfast and dinner at Mrs. Brown's. Her home, a couple blocks from where I lived, was on Gold Avenue one block south of Central Avenue across from the campus. I paid "Ma" Brown, as she was affectionately known among the students, twenty dollars per week for ten meals. I ate there Monday to Friday. Breakfasts were standard but plentiful: juice, cereal (dry or warm), milk, bacon and eggs, and coffee. The evening meals were hardly gourmet, but they were healthy. They varied, depending on the day of the week, from stews, casseroles, enchiladas, chicken, to beef or pork. Vegetables, bread, tea or lemonade, and dessert complemented the meals. (Except for an apple or an orange from Ma Brown's, lunch depended on what I could afford to buy at the Student Union.)

Her makeshift dining room was the perfect place to meet other students. Ma Brown, though quiet and unassuming, was a splendid lady. From time to time she shared humorous stories of former students from Latin America who refused to eat her "peasant" food (i.e., tacos or tamales). Other accounts concerned Albuquerque natives. One local student who allegedly cheated his way in law school became well-known in the community and throughout the state. Overall, students loved Ma Brown.

At midterm, I went to see my advisor Dr. Parish to inquire about grades. There he was bonded behind his wooden desk as though he had never abandoned his office since my initial encounter with him that muggy afternoon in August.

"Good afternoon, Nasario." This time to my amazement he pronounced my name flawlessly and without a hint of formality by invoking Mr. García. "Have a seat," he said, and I sat down as before in the same forsaken and bulky wooden chair. For a fleeting moment I was a tad baffled because of his informality. "I'm looking at your mid-term grades, and they're better than I expected. Here, take a look," and he showed them to me pleased but still sporting a stern look and outward skepticism.

For me there were only two surprises: English and Speech. In Speech I had a B and in English a C. In Spanish and Algebra I had an A and a C, respectively.

All through the semester the north wing of Zimmerman Library (the old section) with its indestructible wooden desks and merciless wooden chairs (I learned to carry a cushion to alleviate the soreness on my butt) became my place of refuge five to six hours per day. The old-fashioned light bulbs hidden under tin shades were hard on the eyes, which added to one's overall tiredness and discomfort.

Of the total daily time in the library, I spent one hour reviewing a booklet on the 1,000 most commonly used and misspelled words. I did my best to learn their spelling as well as to assimilate the meaning, above all those words that sounded alike, for example, *there*, *their*, *they're*. As simplistic as these terms may seem and sound, either I had forgotten their nuances from high school or I never bothered to learn the difference between them. More than once in the confines of the library I shrugged my shoulders with guilt and embarrassment. Aside from the one-hour of trying to rectify certain deficiencies in English, the rest of the time I devoted assiduously to my overall studies.

As the first semester ended, and the marathon hours in Zimmerman Library weighed down on me physically and psychologically, I prepared as best I knew how for final examinations. I enjoyed Speech and Spanish so studying for them was not as stressful as English and Algebra. The latter was a struggle, for sure, but English in a variety of ways was worse. My writing skills and reading comprehension continued to nag me. I fared better in my oral skills, thanks in part to my speech classes.

I completed my first semester with a Grade Point Average

(GPA) of 2.7 on a four-point system. Dr. Parish was surprised, and as nearly as I could ascertain, pleased. As for me, I was content but not overly jubilant since my grades were not outstanding. At the very least I had survived my first semester.

The second semester to some extent resembled the first except that this time I enrolled for fifteen credit hours instead of twelve. And my program of study once again was a combination of required and elective courses.

The long hours and studying routine in Zimmerman Library continued unabated with one notable exception. This time instead of perusing the booklet on 1,000 misspelled words, I revisited my copy of *Harbrace College Handbook* from Mrs. Pigg's class. I was doggedly determined to learn more with regard to the intricacies of grammar, punctuation, diction, and effective use of sentence structure in the hope of passing the English Proficiency Examination.

By the end of the second semester I successfully completed all my courses and was pleased that I had defied my advisor's dire prediction of not lasting more than one semester on campus. But alas I had virtually exhausted all my savings. I did have enough money to pay for my rent in addition to a summer course to offset the three-hour course I did not take the first semester.

In the interim, I learned that my friend Mackey, the retired navy gentleman with whom I worked at Zía Gardens Market prior to my joining the military, was now at Larry's Supermarket on West Central Avenue (old Route 66) across the Río Grande. With his generous help and introduction to Larry Roybal the owner, I was offered a part-time job for the summer. Aside from the much-needed cash, I returned to stocking food shelves, tended to the fruit and vegetable bins, bagged groceries, and cashiered, something I thoroughly enjoyed.

Above all else, I took immense pleasure in meeting and serving customers. Among them were the Unsers, the famous auto-racing couple, and their son Jerry Unser, the Indianapolis race car driver who died in a crash at Indianapolis 500 in 1959 while I worked at Larry's Market. I knew his wife Jeanne who was a customer. Dick Bills and his nephew Glen Campbell, both local favorites at the nearby Hitching Post, were regular customers at Larry's Market. Glen Campbell, singer and song writer, of course, became well-known nationally.

Still lurking in the back of my mind as the summer advanced was the idea, however ill-conceived or asinine, of quitting the university after one year. After all, I could now boast that I had gone to college. At the same time, I was mindful of Mrs. Crossman's words of advice that summer day at Zía Gardens Market regarding the importance of an education. I dared not forget her farsighted advice. I thought of my illiterate parents as well for whom English was not only a foreign language but a challenge as well.

I returned for my sophomore year eager to face new courses, different professors, and unforeseen challenges. But lo and behold I never imagined the array of academic problems that awaited me the next two semesters. My grades plummeted. I struggled mercilessly.

Biology, a four credit-hour course that I took three times, and in which I never earned higher than a D, was the main culprit. In the meantime, I became intrigued with psychology, but any aspirations of majoring in this field were dashed by a young professor in blue denim and white tennis shoes who had just received his doctorate. "I have a consulting business. That's how I earn my living," he said with his feet propped up on his desk. "My teaching salary is poker money," Dumbfounded and aghast by his cynical pronouncements, I not only lost respect for him but failed the course.

Of all the academic challenges I faced, the one perpetual black cloud that hovered over my head was the English Proficiency Examination (EPE). Twice I flunked the seeming unconquerable test with only one attempt left to pass it to become eligible to transfer from the

University College to an upper division and degree granting college. My Remedial English course was only marginally helpful.

As I labored academically, and my savings all but exhausted, I expanded my hours of employment at Larry's Supermarket. I worked on Wednesdays—Doubled S & H green stamp days—as well as ten-hour days on Saturdays and Sundays to pay my rent, meals, tuition, books, and incidentals. Working long hours on weekends gradually began to affect me physically and mentally. By Sunday evening I was exhausted and in no mood to study. The luxury of spending five to six hours of study in the library, as I did my freshman year, was vastly reduced. Poor grades ensued. I accumulated countless hours of D's and F's and was placed on academic probation.

I felt degraded. The day of reckoning and introspection was before me. My future at the university hung in the balance. Hence it was incumbent on me to reassess my work schedule, studying time, as well as my lifestyle. Any further notion of partying at Okie Joe's, a popular hangout on Friday nights on Central Avenue near the university or frequenting the Peacock Nightclub close to Larry's Supermarket on Saturday nights after work, had to be abandoned altogether. As a consequence, I returned to my studying time of several hours at Zimmerman Library. Working at least twenty hours per week and earning two dollars per hour was still necessary to meet my financial obligations.

Three professors, Dr. Albert R. Lopes, Dr. Francis Kercheville, and Ramón J. Sender, encouraged me to pursue a study in languages. The principal motivator was Professor Lopes, my instructor of Beginning Spanish. I recall vividly a brief conversation he and I had at the end of my first semester. "Congratulations!" he said as I headed for the library. "You did well on your final examination. You only missed a couple of accents." "Does that mean I get an A for the course?" I asked kiddingly. This was the beginning of a friendship that lasted for almost forty years until he passed away in 1996 at a local hospital. I believe my wife and I were the last friends to see him the day that he died.

Little did I realize that Spanish, my mother tongue inherently linked to my northern New Mexican roots, would be key to my success as a student and later as a professor. At the same time, my cultural and linguistic background opened the door to the study of several languages. Among them were Portuguese, Italian, and Latin. Having been exposed to a number of European countries (eight total) on my travels during my military duty in Germany undeniably helped me appreciate other languages and cultures.

By now I was in my fourth semester in the University College. The likelihood of transferring to a degree granting college or department unless I passed the nagging English Proficiency Examination looked bleak. Dr. Lopes, with whom I was studying Portuguese, had become my quasi-academic advisor. As the semester was about to end, he said to me, "Tomorrow Counseling and Testing Services is giving the English Proficiency Exam. Show up and take it," he said emphatically.

"It *don't* matter. I can't pass it anyhow," I said, rather disgusted.

"It *do* matter," he snapped at me, "so get over there and take the exam." I did as he admonished me, and by a quirk of fate I passed the nagging and unforgiving test. Dr. Lopes's words were clairvoyant.

"And what do you plan to major in now that you have passed the English Proficiency Exam?" he inquired soon thereafter.

"I have transferred to the College of Education to get a degree in education so I can teach in high school."

"What?" he yelped. "You will do no such thing. Teaching in the public schools is a noble profession, but first you'll major in Spanish and Portuguese. Thereafter you can study for a master's and a doctorate to become a university professor."

My jaw dropped in disbelief, and as a consequence, I reacted rather impetuously, "I can't do that." "Don't tell me you can't do it. I will hear none of that nonsense." Dr. Lopes's scolding words instilled confidence then and throughout my academic career.

Professors Sender and Kercheville completed the triad. Their interests in my education were unmistakable. The latter earned his PhD from the University of Wisconsin and was a specialist in Benito Pérez Galdós, the renowned nineteenth-century Spanish novelist. Galdós became one of my favorite Spanish writers and the subject of my doctoral dissertation.

Ramón Sender an acclaimed Spanish writer escaped the ravages of the Spanish Civil War (1936–1939) under Francisco Franco. I have fond memories of Professor Sender. He was a fascinating and alluring personality. One of the highlights for me as an undergraduate was the two literature courses I studied with him: the Spanish Novel, and Contemporary Spanish Literature. As a result we became acquainted. (I also studied Intermediate Spanish with his wife Florence Hall.)

Sender was formal and rather aloof. Some students—including a number of his colleagues—perceived him as being arrogant. Other individuals considered him an enigma. Deep down he was a complex albeit intriguing personality. What mattered to me is the fact that he didn't mince his words. He called a spade, a spade, "al pan, pan, y al vino, vino."

He used the classroom as a pulpit to vent his anger against his political enemies who impacted his personal life. In the main, the Spanish Civil War comes to mind. Sender's vitriolic words aimed first and foremost at Francisco Franco whose Nationalist forces (Sender was a republican) surfaced from time to time. They murdered his wife Amparo Barayón in Zamora.

Not everything was doom and gloom in his classes. He could be humorous at times. Ernest Hemingway who covered the civil war as a journalist and whom Sender knew did not escape his acerbic remarks either. In seeing artillery fire strike nearby, Hemingway ran for cover under a jeep. Sender described the scene in this fashion. "Hemingway, hombre enorme con una barriga grande, no cupo debajo del vehículo," (Hemingway, a large man with a protruding gut, did not fit hide under the jeep) he said. "Era para reírse uno." (It was enough to make you laugh.)

Levity in Sender's classroom was never lacking. Three times per week as I arrived for class he paced the hallway with hands clasped behind his back and a suit jacket draped over his shoulders. That was typical of men in Spain during the 1950s and 1960s. "Buenos días," he greeted me. "Buenos días a usted profesor," was my cordial response as I walked in the classroom. It was the first day of classes. Everyone was seated. Don Ramón welcomed the students. "Bienvenidos. Primeramente voy a pasar lista" (First I'm going to check roll), he said. "José Armijo, su servidor," and José stood on his feet. He and I were in one of don Ramón's previous classes and such formalities were expected of you. He continued. "Nasario, su servidor," and I rose to my feet.

After don Ramón finished calling roll, he looked at José Armijo a shy individual who was seated toward the front. "Bueno José, ¿cómo se pasó usted el verano?" (Okay José, how did you spend the summer?). Out of the blue, and much to don Ramón surprise, José responded, "Pues yo me pasé el verano deliverando grocerías."

"¡Vaya, vaya! No me diga." (Come now, come now! You don't say), don Ramón remarked somewhat surprised. For us New Mexican Hispanics, we understood perfectly how José had spent the summer, that is, delivering groceries, but to don Ramón, José's words meant that he had spent the summer "deliberating swearwords or vulgarities."

On another occasion an attractive young lady missed an examination. Just before class started, she approached Professor Sender in the hallway about making up the exam. I stood within hearing range and heard their brief exchange. "Profesor, siento que no pudiera tomar el examen el lunes pasado, ¿pero puedo tomarlo el lunes próximo a las nueve?" (Professor, I'm sorry I couldn't take the exam last Monday, but can I take it next Monday at nine o'clock?) With a glow in his eye and a coquettish look don Ramón reacted with a question of his own. ¿Por la noche o por la mañana?" (In the evening or the morning?) Such was his light-hearted side. He was hardly a stuffed shirt.

Professor Sender left the University of New Mexico for California in 1963, the same year I received my master's degree in Portuguese. In 1976 the university bestowed on him an honorary doctorate.

Humorous incidents transpired in other classes as well. A prerequisite for graduate students in one of Professor Kercheville's classes was a presentation on a topic that culminated in a research paper. Most presentations came toward the end of the semester. For a young lady from South America who was married to an American, the day of reckoning had arrived. By now she was quite pregnant. As she spoke with both hands firmly on the podium, she began to grimace and fidget.

Without warning she looked at Professor Kercheville who was in the back of the room, seemingly oblivious to her discomfort, and she said to him, "I think I'm going to have the baby! Should I finish my talk or go to the hospital?"

"For God's sake go to the hospital!" he shouted in a thunderous voice and swiftly jumped to his feet. Her husband, a tall quiet type, rose from his desk and gently accompanied his wife out the classroom. After the baby was born she rejoined her classmates. Everyone applauded and enjoyed a cheerful laugh, including Professor Kercheville.

After the semester ended, graduate students met individually with Professor Kercheville to discuss their research paper and final grade for the course. One female student relayed the ensuing story.

"I went in his office, sat down, and he handed me my term paper. On the front page he had the following grades: Research paper, B+; Classwork, B+; Legs, A+; grade for the course, B+. I then pointed out to the professor, tongue in cheek, of course, that I should have received an A- for the class." The professor's reaction: "Your legs don't average out." They both enjoyed a good chuckle.

The rest of my language professors were rather aloof and preoccupied with their own careers. One notable exception was Sabine R. Ulibarrí, whom many of us called affectionately Uli. He was a charismatic lecturer and a veritable gentleman with whom I studied Introduction to Spanish Literature. Later, after he finished his PhD, he taught Advanced Conversation and Composition. This unlikely course was a dramatic departure from his love of literature. One day in discussing and reviewing *dichos*, folk sayings and other popular expressions, he glanced at the students. In a flirtatious manner he eyed this young lady and said, "Señorita, how do you say in Spanish 'I get on the ball?'" She quickly caught on to his embarrassing trick question, to which the answer was "Yo me pongo en pelota." (I undress myself.) Instead she turned the tables on him and responded, "Póngase usted en peloto." (Strip yourself naked.) The entire class burst out laughing. Uli, a shy man by nature, turned red as a tomato.

Over the years after I left the university Uli and I became good friends. Several times my wife and I visited him and his wife Connie at their home in Albuquerque. On one occasion I went to his office on campus to interview him for my book *Pláticas: Conversations with Hispano Writers of New Mexico*. That's when I learned that he was born in September 1919, the same month and year as my mother. He was touched to learn of the coincidence. I felt a special kinship. Uli died in 2003.

It goes without saying that some professors' words, intended to be comical at times, evoked a snickering or two. Such was the case in my sophomore World Literature course. The instructor was an old bachelor whose misogynistic tendencies were well-known to students. This became patently clear as the semester progressed. As a means of teasing him—some would characterize it as subtle harassment—a group of young females arrived early and occupied the first row of seats in the lecture hall. They proceeded to sit with their legs spread—not crossed—knowing that the professor would take notice. As expected, once he walked in and headed for the podium, he looked out at the throng of students, in particular the young ladies in the front row. The first words to escape his mouth were, "As soon as the gates of hell are closed, I shall begin my lecture." In one swift and synchronized movement, the girls crossed their legs. A chuckle and murmuring reverberated throughout the lecture hall. His metaphorical "gates of hell" did not elude the students.

Back in the 1950s and 1960s attitudes of professors versus students were quite different. Some instructors were prima donnas and thought of themselves as masters in the classroom despite being only fair teachers. And irrespective of the professors' prejudices or pedagogical shortcomings, we students by and large respected them since they were deemed paragons of knowledge.

In spite of encouragement principally from Professor Lopes, I still labored through various science courses. To make matters worse, I got caught at Larry's Supermarket by an unsympathetic union representative. He threatened the owner with a fine if I did not join the Workers' Union. I was laid off work since I could not afford to pay union dues.

Drawing meager unemployment checks not to exceed six weeks was helpful but degrading to my ego. I reported to the State Unemployment Agency weekly to prove that I had looked for a job, which added to my academic and personal pressures. In due course the six-week grace period at the state's unemployment agency expired. I found myself with no income whatsoever and with little cash on reserve.

Eating crackers and pickles for a week at one point was demoralizing, unhealthy, and a low point of my undergraduate days. Nonetheless, I would not burden my parents with my financial plight (they had seven children to feed and clothe). As a last resort, I spoked to Larry at Larry's Market. Given my dilemma he felt compassion and paid the union dues for me to return to work. He knew I was a dependable worker and was glad to have me back at work.

Amid disappointments, perseverance, and dedication throughout my sophomore year, I completed the sixty-hour lower division requirements toward graduation. As an upperclassman I was then able to concentrate on my Spanish major and Portuguese minor. In my junior and senior years I maintained an A- average in all my courses, the antithesis of the first two years of disheartening and mediocre academic performance.

One motivational factor throughout my last two years was the fact that undergraduates like me were in the same classes with graduate students. Some of them were high school teachers enrolled in a program called Master of Arts in Teaching Spanish (MATS). Others were PhD candidates in the School of Inter-American Affairs. I was in awe of their intellectual acumen. Still, I fared well in Spanish and Portuguese, which instilled self-confidence in me.

There were times when I became disenchanted due to the burden of working long hours, finding adequate time to study, and making certain I earned good grades. Even though I was strapped for money, on occasion I visited my father at Crane O'Fallon Company on 612 North First Street where he worked as a laborer. I would invite him to the Excelsior Laundry Cafeteria. I treated him to a cup of coffee and a piece of apple or pumpkin pie, something he thoroughly enjoyed. My visits were uplifting.

On one of our returns to his workplace, he introduced me to Mr. Smith, his boss and office manager who was clad in dress pants, a dress shirt, and a tie. After our encounter, Dad said to me. "Son, get an education so that one of these days you can have an office job just like Mr. Smith." Years later, I kidded my father. "Dad, I did better. I married a Smith!"

For me, languages turned out to be a godsend. Spanish and Portuguese were at the forefront. In addition to these two languages, I studied Italian with Dr. Lopes and Latin with Dr. DeJongh. A frail-looking professor with a degree from Harvard he never failed to wear white gloves in the classroom because he was allergic to chalk.

I am proud to say that being trilingual in English, Spanish, and Portuguese, with a rudimentary ability to converse in Italian, has enabled me to function in a multicultural world. To learn and to know several languages and their respective cultures and literatures is a luxury that propelled me into a multilinguistic and multicultural arena that most Americans don't enjoy.

By the time I finished my undergraduate studies I had earned a BA in Spanish and a minor in Portuguese. Any future success in my post-graduate studies I owe to the superb language training I received in Spanish and Portuguese in the Department of Modern and Classical Languages at the University of New Mexico.

Little did I realize that hot and sultry day in August 1957 when I set foot on campus to meet with my academic advisor, that languages, chiefly among them my New Mexico Spanish language and culture, would be my life's savior in a manner of speaking. As my father who was quite adept at employing folk sayings would have said, "Más vale doblarse que no quebrarse" (It's better to bend than to break). Throughout my undergraduate experience, I may have buckled but I never crumbled.

But there was still more to accomplish as I prepared to enter graduate school.

A New Dawn Arrives

IN JUNE 1962 I GRADUATED with a major in Spanish and a minor in Portuguese even though I had completed all requirements at the end of the fall semester. The milestone was devoid of any fanfare. In fact, I didn't even attend commencement exercises. After what seemed like an endless struggle for five years both academically and financially my energy level was at a low ebb.

My freshman year was encouraging, but being a sophomore proved to be dreadful. The junior and senior years were more inspiring academically and psychologically. Dr. Albert R. Lopes who had become my mentor encouraged me to apply for admittance to graduate school to further my education. I heeded his advice.

I filled out an application form, which was rather straightforward, and addressed a simple letter to the dean of the Graduate School. A transcript of my undergraduate work was required. Within a month I received a letter from the director of admissions informing me of my acceptance to graduate school. I was elated even though I was placed on probationary status. A new dawn had risen.

At the time of the Sputnik era in the 1950s the federal government declared Portuguese a critical language. Hereafter the National Defense Education Act (NDEA) was established and offered graduate fellowships in Portuguese. Dr. Lopes, who had developed outstanding undergraduate and graduate programs in Portuguese, urged me to apply for a NDEA (National Defense Education Act) fellowship to pursue a master's degree in Portuguese.

I filled out multiple forms in addition to procuring three letters of recommendation. Dr. Lopes offered to write one of them.

Without hesitancy I asked Professors Kercheville with whom I had studied several lower and upper division courses. As for the third letter, Dr. Lopes suggested Ramón Sender. "Oh, I can't ask him," I countered without blinking an eye. "And why not?" Dr. Lopes responded. "You've taken classes with him. He's very fond of you," he added.

I went to see Professor Sender in Ortega Hall (the old one) where the language department was housed. I gingerly walked up to his office; the door was ajar. I peered inside. He had his back toward the door. I knocked. He turned around.

"¿Se puede profesor?" (May I come in professor?), I asked.

"Cómo que no. ¡Adelante! ¿Qué tal?" (Of course. Come in! How are you?), he inquired.

"Todo bien" (Everything's okay), I responded. "Vengo a pedirle un favor." (I've come to ask you a favor).

"Por supuesto, Nasario. ¿Qué se te ofrece?" (Of course, Nasario. What can I do for you?)

"Voy a hacer una solicitud para una beca, pero necesito una carta de recomendación. El Profesor Lopes sugirió que viniera a hablar con usted." (I'm going to apply for a scholarship, but I need a letter of recommendation. Professor Lopes suggested I come talk to you.), I said.

"Oh, Nasario, eso de cartas de recomendación yo no sé ni papa, pero escríbela tú y yo la firmo. Oh, ¡no, no, no! Vuelve la semana próxima y ya te tengo una carta lista." (Oh, Nasario, that business of letters of recommendation I don't know beans, but you write it and I'll sign it. Oh, no, no, no! Come back next week, and I'll have a letter ready for you.), he replied.

When I returned the following week, he was looking out the window admiring the New Mexico blue skies and the majestic Sandía Mountains.

"Buenos días, profesor," I said after tapping lightly on the door.

"¡Hola! ¡Adelante!" and he reached and opened the top drawer to his desk. "Aquí tienes la carta. Buena suerte. Espero que mis palabras de apoyo sean de algún valor" (Here's the letter. Good luck. I hope my words of support have some merit), and he handed me an envelope.

"Mil gracias, profesor."

"De nada. A propósito" (You're welcome. By the way), he said, again somewhat informally. "Algún día tú podrías llegar a ser rector de una universidad," and he briefly paused, "lo cual sería una lástima." (One day you could become president of a university, which would be a pity.) (This was tongue in cheek.) Years later I served as assistant vice president of Academic and Student Affairs at the University of Southern Colorado.

In January 1962 I applied for a Foreign Language Fellowship (aka NDEA Fellowship) under the auspices of the National Defense Foreign Language Fellowship Program. The fellowship was sponsored by the Department of Health, Education, and Welfare, Office of Education. A statement of purpose was required in which I was to "Describe and analyze the relations of [my] proposed program to previous education and experience, to further academic plans, and to professional and career goals." I wrote in part, "During my undergraduate course I have become more and more interested in Portuguese and Luso-Brazilian studies. In Graduate School I have decided to concentrate on Luso-Brazilian studies as a major field and to continue my study of Spanish as a minor field so as to be qualified to teach both languages at the college level."

In March I received a letter of award from the Department of Health, Education, and Welfare that stated: "On behalf of the U.S. Commissioner, I am pleased to inform you that you have been awarded a National Defense Foreign Language Fellowship to assist you in preparing yourself to teach the language [Portuguese] specified above in an institution of higher education or for other service of a public nature using the language specified above. Your award is for the PERIOD(S) and at the INSTITUTION(S) [caps. not mine] indicated below."

The NDEA Fellowship was earmarked for the 1962 summer session at the University of Wisconsin—Madison and the academic year 1962–1963 at the University of New Mexico. It goes without saying that I was overjoyed at the unexpected but pleasant news.

The total stipend's award for the summer and academic year, including tuition and travel expenses, was $3,313. My monthly allowance alone was quite lucrative compared to my modest check of forty-plus dollars per week at Larry's Market. I was forever grateful to those professors who supported me for their continuous encouragement and confidence in my ability to succeed in the study of Spanish and Portuguese. I was determined not to disappoint them.

To be awarded the fellowship up to now was one of the happiest moments of my educational career. I would no longer have to work long weekly hours. And to be able to spend more time in Zimmerman Library devoted to my studies was a blessing. After working five years (1957–1962) at Larry's Market I offered my sincere thanks to Larry, said goodbye to Frank Farris, the manager, and I quit at the end of the spring semester.

In June I journeyed to the University of Wisconsin—Madison for the summer session. A small group of my classmates, Bill Harrison among them, joined Dr. Albert R. Lopes who was invited as a visiting professor of Portuguese. Bill Harrison, a close friend of mine, hailed from Storm Lake, Iowa. We decided to form a two-car caravan for our long trip across Texas and the Midwest. From Albuquerque he and his wife and kids rode in their car, and I drove my 1954 Chevrolet. We traveled all the way to Bill's hometown, but spent one night in Stillwater, Oklahoma, with an aunt of his before we reached Storm Lake where his wife and kids stayed. Bill and I then departed in my car for Madison.

Shortly after our arrival we rented a basement apartment from an elderly lady in the countryside, about twenty to thirty minutes from campus. Our classes were in Bascom Hall, a keystone and unmistakable building that was the hub of the university.

A reception was hosted on campus in the Union Memorial Building shortly after our arrival in honor of the New Mexico contingency. The get-together turned out to be very special since that is where I met Janice Smith, my future wife, who coincidentally hailed from Albuquerque. She was finishing her master's degree in Portuguese, awarded to her at the end of the summer session while I was still in Madison. In fact, Dr. Lopes served on her master's oral examination committee alongside Dr. Lloyd Kasten, professor of Portuguese at the University of Wisconsin. Both professors with highly respected programs were looked up as iconic promoters of Portuguese in this country.

The summer session ended. I enjoyed my two courses and meeting classmates from different parts of the United States. To attend a Big Ten university was a sobering experience for someone like me who was raised in rural New Mexico. On September 20, 1962, I received a letter from L. H. Adolfson, director of The University of Wisconsin-Summer Sessions congratulating me on my academic success. His letter was a capstone to an enjoyable summer at the university.

But the most exciting time was courting my future wife, Janice Smith. In the confines of Lake Mendota and University Bay we strolled peacefully on Lakeshore Path, totally oblivious to passersby, surfing ferry boats, or young people paddling their kayaks. Those environs and romantic moments are still indelibly fixed in my mind. My summer days in Madison were magical, serendipitous in fact; they were to steer me in a new and exciting direction in my life.

Yet, there was a fly in the ointment, so to speak, since Jan, as I came to call her, had decided to go back to Brazil. She had previously spent six months in Rio de Janeiro and six months in Bahia on a cultural exchange scholarship, but this time she was to return to Brazil with the Peace Corps.

I proceeded home to Albuquerque after summer school ended with an intermittent stop at Kansas State University in Manhattan to visit Jan where the Peace Corps trainees were prepared for their tour of duty in Brazil. From Manhattan I continued my journey home. I arrived in Albuquerque in late July. By now the Peace Corps trainees were at the University of Oklahoma in Norman, the penultimate stopover before they departed the United States. I visited Jan there with our future hanging in the balance. Either she went to Brazil with the Peace Corps, or we became husband and wife. We were married in October 1962 and recently celebrated our 61st wedding anniversary.

With my NDEA fellowship in hand for the AY 1962–1963, it was a joy not having to work long hours taking care of fruit and vegetable bins, sacking groceries, and cashiering. After all of the trials and tribulations of earning a bachelor's degree, I had an epiphany. Besides, I had my beloved wife for moral support.

The academic year progressed rather nicely. I completed all prerequisites for a master's degree in Portuguese. They included a battery of Portuguese and Spanish courses, plus I passed the graduate language examination in Italian. The penultimate requirement was the thesis. I conducted a comparative study titled "Religious and Liberal Thoughts in Eça de Queiroz and Benito Pérez Galdós," the latter Spanish and the former Portuguese, both nineteenth-century master novelists. Lastly, I appeared before a committee of Professors Albert Lopes, Chairman, Francis Kercheville, and Sabine Ulibarrí for an oral defense of the thesis. The question-and-answer session went smoothly; it culminated in six unforgettable but rewarding years at the University of New Mexico.

In the spring of 1963, six years after I met with Dr. William J.

Parish, my freshmen advisor, commencement exercises were held at Johnson Gymnasium. By now Dr. Parish, the dean of the Graduate School, was offering congratulations and handing out master's and PhD diplomas the evening of graduation. As I approached the platform to receive my master's certificate in Portuguese—the first student to receive a master's degree in Portuguese at the University of New Mexico according to Dr. Lopes—Dr. Parish was surprised to see me. "What in the hell are you doing here?" he said with a wry smile as he handed me my diploma.

That moment was the crowning glory for all the hard work and sacrifices I had made the past six years. I walked away proudly and muttered under my breath, "I taught you, you bastard." Dr. Parish's harsh, disconcerting, and pessimistic words that hot summer day in 1957 came alive when he said to me, "Son, your test scores are so far below the national average, I doubt that you'll last more than one semester on this campus." In retrospect, his words were a great source of motivation to prove him wrong—and I did! But let me be clear. I did not earn two degrees on my own. There were those benevolent individuals on campus who both guided and encouraged me on my educational journey. I have never forgotten them, above all Dr. Lopes.

Prior to finishing my master's in Portuguese, the University of New Mexico was selected as a Latin American Peace Corps Training Center for volunteers going to Brazil. In 1963–1964 my wife and I joined a group of instructors who taught Portuguese to those trainees destined for Brazil. Though a neophyte in pedagogy my first teaching venture in time led to a career of thirty-six years as a university professor. What a wonderful beginning! Meeting young and idealistic Peace Corps trainees from elite institutions such as Harvard, Temple University, and elsewhere emboldened me to continue my education.

As my wife and I were on the cusp of fulfilling our teaching contract, I had to decide on a PhD program and university suitable to my interests and needs. In discussing my educational future with Dr. Lopes, my erstwhile advisor, he suggested that I contact the University of Texas at Austin because of a well-known Luso-Brazilian scholar in the Department of Spanish and Portuguese. I received neither an acknowledgment nor a response to my letter of inquiry. Dr. Lopes's reaction was short and to the point. "It's their loss."

At his suggestion I decided to pursue a doctorate in Spain. He recommended the University of Granada. Because we had never been to Spain, it would be a new adventure for me and my wife. An array of unforeseen and unknown surprises awaited us, but we were young, adventurous, and even bold. I welcomed the challenge. Further, I had my wife, highly intelligent and a pillar of strength and support.

Time, the determiner of all things, would tell the tale. Spain, my *madre patria*, the motherland across the Atlantic waters was to be our home for fifteen months. "Dreams can only come true if you dare to pursue them," I thought to myself. My beloved maternal grandmother's simple but powerful words rang loud and clear. "El que no mira pa delante, atrás se queda." (He who doesn't look toward the future, lags behind.)

Granada

Faraway but at Home

IN EARLY MARCH 1964 MY Jan and I boarded a Trans World Airlines (TWA) airplane at the old Albuquerque Airport destined for Granada in southern Spain. This was our first trip of many future journeys to the Iberian Peninsula. Twenty-four-hours later we landed at the Barajas Airport in Madrid. At first glance it was not only small but extremely depressing. Once inside the terminal the bulky and uncomfortable dark wooden benches did little to ease the glumness and discomfort. And the prolonged wait for our plane to Granada exacerbated our anxiety. I wondered in silence what might await us beyond the drabness that permeated the airport during the Francisco Franco era.

Our plane bound for Granada accommodated no more than eight passengers, but it was half empty. The bumpy ride took about an hour to an hour and a half. The Granada airport south of the city was small with a short runway but amply suitable for small planes.

From there my wife and I fetched the only taxi parked outside the terminal that was no more than a large two-story house. "¿Pa ónde, señorehs?" (Where to?) he asked, stressing the last syllable, our opening introduction to the local dialect. "Para el centro de Granada" (To downtown Granada), I responded.

After his initial query the driver didn't utter a single word until we reached downtown. Along the way he honked his horn almost incessantly. Out of curiosity I stole a look through the windshield from the backseat to see if there was livestock on the road. I saw nothing that would prompt him to press on his horn. Once we arrived at the hotel in the center of town, I paid the driver and tipped him a few pesetas. Standing beside our luggage in front of the hotel before we entered to inquire about a room, my wife asked, "Honey, why did he keep honking? What was he honking at?"

"Who knows?" I answered.

Months later, true or not, someone provided an answer: "Oh, it's just a habit, an obsession taxi drivers have once they get behind the steering wheel in the countryside. They pretend or imagine that cows or donkeys are on the road just to show off and catch people's attention. It's pure silliness, *tonterías*."

Following two nights in a hotel, plus getting slightly acquainted with Granada's downtown coffee shops, bars, and restaurants, we looked up Bob Duncan who had been my phonetics instructor at the University of New Mexico. He was in Granada on sabbatical with his wife Nina; both were staying at the Fabiola, a local pension. At their suggestion we rented a room there that was cheaper than a hotel but still expensive for our budget. A light breakfast (Spaniards, unlike Americans, we discovered rather quickly, did not eat a hearty breakfast) and lunch were included in the daily room charge.

Early one morning after breakfast I walked to the post office across from our hostel to rent a mailbox where we could receive our mail from the United States. My trip turned out to be a learning experience. Several things are worth noting that may be of interest to the reader. First, I was directed by a guard in a gray uniform to consult with a gentleman at the end of this cavernous hall. The old fellow sporting a dark blue suit with gold-colored buttons sat at an inauspicious wood desk. He resembled a hotel porter but was more unkempt. His outfit I learned and witnessed as time elapsed was typical among state employees (most of them males) under the Franco regime.

Another thing that attracted my attention and piqued my curiosity was the gentleman's Spanish. I greeted him politely, "Buenos días señor. Me gustaría alquilar un buzón" (Good morning sir. I would like to rent a mailbox), and he responded rapidly in what to me was totally incomprehensible Spanish. He then handed me a blank form, which I filled out and returned to him. I paid him a modest rental fee. He in return gave me a key and a receipt with a number (*Apartado* 411) to my private mailbox. I pondered for a fleeting moment what he had said in his local vernacular.

I realized rather quickly in conversing with newspaper vendors and waiters at cafes and restaurants that the Granadino dialect in many respects had a life of its own. A gentleman at the newspaper kiosk would say, "Bueno diah. ¿Co' 'stá 'te? ¿En qué poo servile?" Transliteration, "Buenos días. ¿Cómo está usted? ¿En qué puedo servirle?" (Good morning. How are you? What can I do for you?) His words were a perfect example, a microcosm, in fact, of the linguistic idiosyncrasies of the local Spanish. I could recite numerous other samples, but suffice it to say that one of the common quirks in pronunciations was to drop the final "s" of certain plural words and then open and stress the last syllable. Case in point, *buenas* or *cosas* became *buená* or *cosá*.

One could hear a more standard Spanish among university professors and students who were not Granadinos. There was a professor born in Granada who taught art history; his Spanish was difficult to comprehend. Coincidentally, the pronunciation of some Spanish words were similar to those I heard and learned as a child (e.g., *servile > servirle*, *poo > puedo*, *naa > nada*). Being able to communicate in Spanish, my native language of northern New Mexico with strong linguistic and cultural roots to Spain, Andalucía in particular, I felt a certain kinship. This added to my comfort even though the Granadino vernacular at times was a challenge, but within time my oral comprehension improved.

A day or so after our arrival in Granada, we purchased a book of black and white photos by Francisco Prieto-Moreno titled *Granada* (it's still part of our library holdings on Spain) in which he described the city's splendor and allure. I soon heard a heart-warming and popular saying that truly pierces your soul once you've gotten acquainted with Granada's beauty and magic. The expression goes something like this in Granadino Spanish, "No hay naa más triste que ser uno ciego en Graná." (There is nothing sadder than to be blind in Granada.) Other versions exist such as "Dale limosna, mujer, que no hay en la vida nada, como la pena de ser ciego en Granada." (Be charitable, my lady, for there is nothing sadder in life than to be blind in Granada.)

I would like to add parenthetically that those poignant words reminded me of my maternal great-grandmother (we called her *Mamá* Juanita) who was totally blind and derived utmost pleasure from smoking. As a small boy I rolled and lit her cigarettes so she wouldn't burn her lips.

After the Prieto-Moreno book I bought and read the highly acclaimed *Tales of the Alhambra*, a collection of essays regarding the Moors and Spaniards by Washington Irving (1783–1859). He's the American writer who stayed at the Hotel Alhambra Palace while he wrote his work. A nearby hotel, the Washington Irving that still exists, was later named in his honor.

Jan and I spent the next two months slowly warming up to Granada our home for the next year or so with intermittent stays in Madrid and Lisbon. Our arrival in March 1964 coincided with the Lenten Season. From the hostel we could see on top of a building not far off from our dining room a statue of Isabel la Católica, Queen of Spain (1451–1504). We could also observe every evening at dusk from our room the elaborate religious processions aligned with *pasos*, colorful religious floats of differing sizes. One carried San Cecilio the local patron saint; other floats included statues from churches within the community. Earnest devoutness was exhibited by none other than groups of women wearing long black mantillas as they walked, prayed, and sang religious songs.

This display of religiosity coupled with the singing of hymns immediately reminded me of my paternal grandmother back at our own village of Guadalupe (Ojo del Padre) in the Río Puerco Valley of New Mexico. The firsthand connection between Granada and Guadalupe, two faraway communities, made my heart and soul happy. I felt an instantaneous and special affinity.

The highpoint of the Lenten Season of course was Holy Week. For Granadinos to attend Mass in the Cathedral brought to a climax the forty days of prayer, repentance, and abstinence that started with Ash Wednesday.

The Royal Chapel too palpitates with Spain's dramatic past. Here is where the Reyes Católicos, Catholic Monarchs, Fermando and Isabel, are entombed. They epitomize a monumental slice of history—the expulsion of the Moors from Granada in 1492 and sub-sequent unification of Spain—that evokes pride among the locals and enthralls visitors as well.

Adjacent to the Cathedral is the Alcaicería, the medieval Moorish marketplace. Today the tourist mecca is abuzz daily with activity irrespective of the seasons of the year. There you can buy an assortment of items ranging from a simple trinket to an expensive handmade flamenco dress (cheaper ones imported from China are also available).

The Plaza Bib-Rambla, a short distance from the Cathedral, had a *chocolatería* in the 1960s known for its delicious hot chocolate and churros (fried-dough pastry). My wife and I went there periodically on Sundays to drink the thick-hot chocolate and churros for break-fast, a delectable treat indeed and a tradition among Granadinos.

Once the Lenten celebrations ended, we moved to a less ex-pensive hostel situated near Puerta Real, the center of town. From here I walked a few blocks, or *cuadras*, down Calle de Fuentezuelas to the Facultad de Filosofía y Letras (Humanities Building) of the University of Granada. There located not far from the main campus students took courses in the humanities. I inquired about enrolling for classes in the spring semester but was informed that classes had started in February. I was deeply disappointed since I would have to wait until August to register for the fall semester. Besides, in order to pursue a doctorate in Spanish language and literature, the main reason for going to Spain, I had to procure a *covalidación*, validation from the Ministry of Education in Madrid.

For the time being Jan and I learned to adjust to our new modest living quarters that consisted of a large room with a terrace that overlooked a small plaza. The large room had a bed, a living area, and a sink with hot and cold water but no bathroom. Instead, as the concierge advised us, we had to use a communal bathroom "down the hall." The first morning I went to use the bathroom three young men were waiting in line with tissue in one hand and a towel draped over their left or right shoulder. This scene was the first anomaly, a cultural awakening in fact, but there would be other incongruities that my wife and I had to adapt to as we settled in Granada.

Our daily room and board included breakfast and the noon meal, the main meal of the day. For dinner my wife and I ventured out to *la calle*, the street, as the Spaniards say, for tapas and a beverage or we purchased snacks at a small food store to eat in our room.

Unlike Americans, including us New Mexicans who eat a hearty breakfast, the Spaniards seemed to be on the run and only ate *pan tostado*, toast, and *café con leche*, coffee with milk. As a kid at the ranch I had my share of coffee and milk. I was used to the combination. All in all, my wife and I had to get accustomed to the Andalusian cuisine.

Eating the Spanish tortilla (potatoes and onions omelet) and fish virtually every other day comprised part of our diet. Being from New

Mexico and consuming fish was a new dietary experience, but what I could never relish was to be served the whole fish with the tail stuck in its mouth. I found that a bit unsightly and repulsive. Beef and chicken were expensive and rarely on the menu, but every so often my wife and I ate at a popular restaurant where we ordered *pollo al ajo*, garlic chicken that we thoroughly enjoyed. Oddly enough the eating place was called Restaurante Sevilla.

We continued to explore Granada where Federico García Lorca, the renowned Spanish poet and member of a group of poets known as the Generation of '27, made his home before his demise. Lorca was born in Fuente Vaqueros a few kilometers west of Granada. He also attended the University of Granada.

Near our pension I discovered a park named in honor of Mariana Pineda, a local heroine, revolutionist, and liberal, who was born in Granada (1804–1831). In terms of her personal ideology, Mariana Pineda was years ahead of her time. García Lorca, a playwright in his own right, eulogized her in a play titled *Mariana Pineda*.

As my wife and I strolled through the streets of Granada, we came upon the name of Angel Ganivet an intellectual and philosopher born in Granada whom I was familiar with. He belonged to the Generation of '98 and is best known for his work *Idearium español*.

I learned of other literary notables in the region who were not Spaniards. One was an Englishman, Gerald Brenan, who at the time was living in Yegen, a village in the region of the Alpujarras in the Granada province southeast of the city. He was a prominent Hispanist whose work *The Literature of the Spanish People* I had read in my literature courses at the University of New Mexico. By all accounts no foreigner at that time was better versed on Spanish literature, Spain's history, and the Spaniards' way of life than Brenan. His books, *The Spanish Labyrinth* and *South from Granada* that I read as well prior to arriving in Granada, further attest to his intimate knowledge of Spain.

Even Ernest Hemingway left an imprint on Granada. He had his favorite bar (I don't recall the name) on Calle de Recogidas. Whenever he was in town, he indulged in *pinchitos*, small cubes of charcoaled pork or chicken complemented by wine. Photographs of Hemingway were posted on the wall behind the bar. My wife and I went there on special occasions and treated ourselves to pinchitos; they were indeed delectable.

A leisurely stroll from the center of town alongside the Darro River was remarkable. Far beyond the countless shops and bars that line the river on one side and the colorful multistory homes on the other, decorated beautifully during the Corpus Christi fiestas in June, one comes upon the Arabic baths. Farther away are the popular Gypsy Caves. There the *gitanos* with their tantalizing flamenco dances entertain curious tourists from Europe, the United States, and elsewhere. The women dressed in beautiful floor-length flamenco dresses dazzle the visitors with their *zapateaos*, heel-kicking rhythmic sounds, amid musicians enthusiastically strumming their guitars. The more versatile and talented Gypsies migrate to larger cities like Madrid and Sevilla in search of universal stardom.

Before reaching the Gypsy Caves there is the Albaicín (also spelled Albayzín), whose legacy dates back to Moorish medieval times and the Nasrid Kingdom of Granada. Across the Darro River from the heights of the Albaicín one is awestruck by the majestic beauty of the Alhambra palace and fortress that was declared a World Heritage Site in 1984, twenty years after my wife and I first arrived in Granada.

Prieto-Moreno's book mentioned earlier with its stark black and white photos conveyed, as I learned day by day, Granada's magnificence. But the photographs hardly do justice to the beauty and magic of the Alhambra and Generalife (summer palace of the Nasrid rulers of the Emirate of Granada) adorned with splendid royal palaces, lively water fountains, and elaborate gardens. The snow-capped

Sierra Nevada that looms in the distance behind the Alhambra captures one's eye-popping attention. The imposing and unforgettable beauty of the Sierra Nevada and the Alhambra palace and fortress to this day are embedded in my heart and soul.

A romantic getaway to the Alhambra at dusk whether in the spring or summer for young people like me and my wife (we were both in our twenties) or older couples as well was heavenly. Twice a month, the 1st and 15th, the Alhambra was lit at dusk for several hours, but rarely did we see more than a handful of couples meander throughout the gardens enjoying the musical sounds of flowing water. Nowadays, because of its universal popularity, the Alhambra is aglow more frequently and besieged in the summer with hordes of people jostling each other. Those romantic evenings of yore in seeming solitude and tranquility that my wife and I enjoyed in 1964–1965 are gone forever.

On one of romantic visits to the Alhambra, we leisurely strolled throughout the colorful gardens. Water cascaded nearby; it broke the stillness of the moment as we descended these step stones. When we reached the bottom of the steps, there stood a caretaker.

"¡Buenas!" he said.

"Buenas," I responded.

"Es aquí en estos escalones donde el poeta Juan Ramón Jiménez escribió alguna de su poesía" (It is here at these steps where the poet Juan Ramón Jiménez composed some of his poetry), he explained.

I was intrigued by his spontaneous and proud revelation. He proceeded to tell us that the eminent Spanish poet once requested permission—and was granted—for the entire Alhambra to be closed so that he could compose some of his poetry in solitude. True or not, it was an alluring tale that befitted the tranquil atmosphere and musically flowing waters of the Alhambra.

After two months in Granada, we departed for Madrid in May 1964 and later Lisbon, but we returned to Granada in late summer for me to attend the university. In the capital we stayed at the Pensión Clariz on Carrera de San Jerónimo virtually next door to the Palacio de las Cortes where the Spanish Congress holds its meetings. Though expensive for our budget, the Clariz was within walking distance to Puerta del Sol, the hub of downtown Madrid, Plaza de España, the Museo del Prado, and the Parque del Buen Retiro. The Biblioteca Nacional de España, the National Library of Spain, was farther away but still within a reasonable distance on foot.

In Madrid I inquired at the Ministry of Education, as advised at the University of Granada, regarding the requirements for a *doctorado*. Back in Granada I received a disconcerting letter. I was informed that since there was no reciprocity or memorandum of understanding between institutions of higher learning in the United States and Spain, I would have to start as a first-year undergraduate student. I wrote a letter to the Ministry of Education and expressed my disappointment. An angry response followed from a gentleman stating in effect, "rules are rules." I did pay five hundred pesetas (about fifty dollars) for the *convalidación*, validation that permitted me to register for graduate courses (*cursos monográficos*) as a foreign student at the University of Granada.

I learned during the fifteen months in Spain that the most minute and quasi-official enterprise required *póliza(s)*, stamp or stamps. These bureaucratic niceties were mandated by the Spanish government or local officials. At best said stamps were somewhat analogous to a legal or quasi-legal document by a notary public in this country.

While in Madrid I decided to continue my research on Benito Pérez Galdós the renowned nineteenth-century Spanish novelist who comprised part of my master's thesis. (Eça de Queiroz, the celebrated Portuguese novelist from Leiria north of Lisbon was the other writer.) My first visit to the Biblioteca Nacional to procure a library card turned into a bureaucratic boondoggle because of being a foreigner. I finally went to the United States Embassy and obtained without difficulty a Letter of Introduction that enabled me to secure a card to use the library facilities (there were some restrictions but no fees).

One or two of the ever-present elderly gentlemen in blue suits and gold-plated buttons informed me that resources regarding Galdós were meager and virtually nonexistent. (I wondered silently how a custodian was privy to this information.) I was then directed to the Ateneo de Madrid.

The Ateneo, a cultural repository on Calle del Prado, was a scant two blocks from our Pensión Clariz. Famous writers known as Ateneístas at one time frequented the Ateneo. Among them were Galdós himself, Emilia Pardo Bazán, Miguel de Unamuno, and Valle Inclán. Not much information on Galdós was available at the Ateneo either. Further research would have to wait until I pursued a doctorate in the United States.

After a month in Madrid, my wife and I settled in Lisbon for two months at the Pensao Santa Catarina. In Portugal both of us were able to practice our Portuguese. We also visited Sintra, Oporto, Coimbra, and Leiria where Eça de Queiroz's classic novel *O Crimen do Padre Amaro* takes place. His masterpiece, too, as mentioned earlier, was a central focus of my Master thesis at the University of New Mexico.

Prior to leaving for Madrid and Lisbon, we made arrangements to live with Mercedes Garoffolo in the Albaicín, the medieval Moorish district of Granada. Robert Duncan and his wife Nina, mentioned earlier in this narrative, introduced us to Mercedes from Albuquerque who now made Granada her home. We returned in August from Lisbon and paid Mercedes Garoffolo room and board (only breakfast and lunch were included) throughout the academic year, 1964–1965. She and her three children, two young daughters and a son, lived in the Carmen de San Gregorio (i.e., a large house with a beautiful garden) that she rented. Mercedes was a widow whose husband Vincent had been a professor at the University of New Mexico before he passed away. From the luscious garden of our new domicile, we could see the Sacromonte, the Gypsies' primary environs, as well as the snow-capped Sierra Nevada that flaunted its magnificent beauty year-round.

About a ten-minute walk from Mercedes's Carmen was the Plaza of San Nicolás. My wife and I took a stroll there at least once a week. On the way we walked alongside the enclosed and purportedly historic private home of the famous Spanish composer Manuel de Falla who lived there in the 1920s and 30s. Once at San Nicolás, we enjoyed the breathtaking views of the Alhambra and its surroundings: the Generalife, the Carlos V Palace, and the Patio de los Arrayanes.

Once the semester started, I meandered my way from Mercedes's place via the Albaicín down to the Carrera del Darro, a brisk fifteen-minute walk, and headed for the university. I walked toward the heart of downtown until I reached the Facultad de Filosofía y Letras for my *cursos monográficos* (doctoral courses). The last stretch took about twenty minutes. For nine months these were my daily treks except during inclement weather. If the frigid winter mornings were unbearable, I rode the city bus roundtrip.

The Albaicín's narrow and winding walkways and smooth stone steps on an incline were a challenge. By the end of the academic year (1964–1965) I was familiar with all the stone walkways, food stores, nooks and crannies, and shortcuts. Some of the elderly women who used the same paths on their daily shopping sprees at open markets near the Darro River or at stores in the Albaicín sooner or later recognized me. Their friendly and quick morning salutation, "Adió" (hello, good morning, and goodbye all in one swoop), greeted me. I felt like a good neighbor and not just a stranger or passerby, a compliment to them indeed since the Granadino though differential tended to be somewhat aloof and not easy to befriend.

This standoffishness is not unique or indigenous solely to Granada. In Gerald Brenan's *South from Granada* one learns that unfriendliness is common and self-contained within the small villages of Yegen, where Brenan lived, and Ugíjar and Órgiva, all situated in the Alpujarra province of Granada. Yet paradoxically whenever there are fiestas in either village, the surrounding neighbors are invited to participate in the celebrations. This type of cordiality is made manifest in Granada as well when the Corpus Christi fiestas are held in June. Villagers from the outlying areas are welcome to participate in the festivities.

The lack of friendliness was also true of my classmates at the university, with one rare exception. I befriended César López González, but his home was Cartagena in eastern Spain. He subsequently married an American, earned a master's and a PhD in Spanish from the University of Southern California, and taught at Scripps College until he retired a few years ago. We remain friends to this day.

The most vivid recollection I have of my first days at the University of Granada as I stepped inside the Humanities Building was the smell of garlic. Eating *pan tostado al ajo*, garlic toast, for breakfast was customary. But the cigarette smoke that clouded the hallways as students paced back and forth, chatting and puffing on their Celtas (popular Spanish cigarettes) before classes started, too, was a revelation to me. Many students in the Humanities perceived their own role in a rather lackadaisical manner bereft of any ironclad goals in mind. Little by little I got acclimated to the atmosphere and overall educational environment in a Spanish university.

Back in the 1960s professors in Spain for the most part were held in high esteem. Some of them were less inclined to be devoted teachers and/or good scholars because of their meager salaries. My academic advisor was a case in point. After he taught his classes, he moonlighted as a baker to augment his low salary even though he held the *cátedra*, or tenure, a prestigious position at that time.

There were exceptions, of course. Manuel Alvar, the eminent linguistics instructor, was a prime example. Dr. Alvar, unlike some of his colleagues, was an anomaly. He was a dedicated and demanding teacher and a serious scholar. His reputation among students was well-known. He arrived promptly on time and taught the full fifty minutes or an hour and fifteen minutes, depending on the length of class time. Other less serious professors showed up late and dismissed classes early. Alvar's possible no-nonsense attitude stemmed in part from being a visiting professor at the University of California at Santa Barbara. He marveled and talked about his positive experience there because students were more diligent.

For the fall semester the only graduate or doctoral course available was in linguistics that Dr. Alvar taught. I don't know how many post-graduate students besides me were in his class. For sure I was the only student from the United States. Most undergraduate students, and maybe some graduates, scoffed at Alvar because he was stringent and took his teaching seriously.

Nothing was more telling than the first time I took an examination in one of his classes, proctored by a teaching assistant. Several classmates, mostly underclassmen I would surmise, and possibly even some graduate students, resorted to what were called *chuletas*, a euphemism for cheating tablets. Students secretly carted them to class but were used indiscreetly. While they took the exam, I could not help but notice an assortment of paper shuffling and note sharing. The constant chatter added to the crescendo of noise most of which the teaching assistant ignored.

One of the cleverest cheating "techniques" that I witnessed was a young lady who wore black high-top boots to class and sat by the window. As the sun shone on the boots I could see a variety of purple-like scribblings on her boots as she moved them back and forth or up and down for her notes to reflect against the sun. It was an ingenious approach to cheating, to say the least.

I often felt that students spent more time concocting cheating schemes than they did preparing for a test. But then again, it was games students played. In some cases the assistant who proctored the exams may have been privy to the questions in advance and then shared them with friends in the class as he sat at the professor's desk seemingly oblivious to the ongoing hubbub. I doubt seriously that Professor Alvar's assistant shared questions in advance with the students, although arrogance and disrespect appeared to have no boundaries.

This certainly appeared to be true in a class on the History of Spain that I audited. After the first examination the professor scolded the students, "¡Vaya! Pues cayeron varios exámenes perfectos. Desaprobados ¡Todos!" He no doubt was keenly aware of the cheating shenanigans.

The consensus among most students in the humanities seemed to be, especially the female students, that attending the university was more of a pastime than a serious pedagogical undertaking. They viewed their role as social entertainment rather than an exercise in learning, above all since tuition was relatively inexpensive. The underhandedness during examinations tended to bear out their attitudes and pronouncements.

The linguistic class with Dr. Alvar and the history course I audited in the fall semester were a perfect way to get acclimated to a Spanish university in general and the classrooms, professors, and classmates in particular.

Before long the spring semester had arrived. By then my wife and I had begun to worry about our financial situation. Not knowing what we were to do for income once we returned to the United States was rather unsettling. The thought of returning to Albuquerque to work at a supermarket, something I did and enjoyed from junior high until I received my bachelor's degree, was not very appealing.

Then lo and behold as if by the stroke of a magic wand we received a letter dated January 11, 1965, from Jack E. Tomlins. He was professor of Spanish at Chatham College in Pittsburgh. My wife and I met him the summer of 1963 at the Latin American Peace Corps Training Center of the University of New Mexico when all three of us taught Portuguese. He wanted to know when we planned to return to the United States. A position in Spanish for the fall semester at Chatham College was imminent should I be interested (more in chapter 8).

From then on I concentrated more calmly on my three spring semester doctoral courses: a linguistic course with Manuel Alvar (a sequel to semester one); and two graduate seminars. One was on Luis de Góngora, the Baroque lyric poet of the Siglo de Oro, Spanish Golden Age, taught by Emilio Orozco Díaz. The other seminar related to the Renaissance poet Garcilaso de la Vega. Antonio Gallego Morell, a Garcilaso specialist, was the instructor.

Both Orozco Díaz, a highly respected Góngora scholar, and Gallego Morell who enjoyed a respectable level of prominence himself, were serious teachers. Orozco Díaz, though not in the best of health, and Gallego Morell who at that time (1965) was the mayor of Granada (years later he was named the rector of the university), never failed to show up to teach their weekly seminars. Both came to class well-prepared and engaged the students in provocative and introspective discussions. They were consummate professionals in discharging their teaching duties.

The students in both seminars, all of whom were Spaniards, were intelligent and articulate. As a foreign student in my corduroy jacket (unbeknownst to me, only country bumpkins wore this type of jacket in southern Spain at that time), shirt, and necktie, I stood out like a sore thumb. (Most students dressed casually but neatly.) In due course, the students along with the professors found out that I was from Albuquerque. The historical, cultural, and linguistic affinity between Spain and New Mexico was an asset. Because of this kinship, I was at ease and also never felt intimidated in class discussions in large measure due to the excellent training I received in languages at the University of New Mexico.

Toward the end of the semester—the first week in June—I submitted my research papers to Professors Orozco Díaz and Gallego Morell. Aside from attending classes, reading assignments, and class discussions, the research papers were the principal requisites for the course. The seminar papers in concert with Manuel Alvar's final examination in linguistics culminated in the four *cursos monográficos* that I enrolled for during 1964–1965. To this day I treasure those days at the Facultad de Filosofía y Letras. They were enriching both culturally and academically.

I waited five weeks instead of two as I had anticipated before I departed from Granada. I had to consult with my professors, in particular Orozco Díaz and Gallego Morell, to make certain that my two research papers were acceptable.

Next, I traveled to Stockholm to rejoin my wife who in early June went to visit her sister Jeanne and family in Sweden. Eager to see my wife, the rollicking three-day train trip from Spain to Sweden at times seemed dreary and never-ending. After leaving Stockholm, we visited Copenhagen, Frankfurt, Brussels, and Amsterdam before we boarded a ship across the White Cliffs of Dover on our way to London. We returned to Albuquerque in July 1965 to prepare for our long journey by car to Pittsburgh. I was eager to embark on my teaching career at Chatham College.

Postscript

In June of 2013 my wife and I revisited Granada for the second or third time since my university days of 1964–1965. We stayed at Mercedes Garoffolo's new home in the Albaicín where we visited her years earlier while she was still alive. This time we were the guests of Vicente, her grandson, and María, Mercedes's daughter. Vicente is the caretaker of the beautiful home whereas María, his mother, lives with her family in Utrera not far from Sevilla.

Our return to Granada, the city endowed with everlasting beauty, was nostalgic and a bit anticlimactic. Mercedes Garoffolo's home in the Albaicín enjoys a breathtaking view of the Alhambra and the Sierra Nevada. The Albaicín, like some of the sites that we became accustomed to back in 1964–1965, had changed dramatically in forty-plus years. Granada's overall population, too, had grown by leaps and bounds.

On a bright sunny day we walked to what used to be the Facultad de Filosofía y Letras (now the Center for Foreign Students.). Revisiting the Humanities Building brought back myriad remembrances— among them the smell of garlic toast in the morning before classes started. Except for the name change of the Humanities Building, the inside looked as though time had stood still. Nothing had changed. I visited Classroom 11 of the eminent linguist Dr. Manuel Alvar my former linguistics professor. His desk and those of the students were in the same place. It was an eerie and sobering experience but fulfilling, nonetheless.

After Alvar left the University of Granada and moved to Madrid, he taught at the Universidad Complutense de Madrid and the Universidad Autónoma de Madrid. From 1988–1991, he was named director of the prestigious Real Academia Española. In the meantime, we had exchanged periodic Christmas greetings.

In 1991, while in Madrid, I spoke with him on the telephone about getting together, but he was scheduled to deliver a lecture in Logroño. Being that he was very fond of the Colonial Spanish of northern New Mexico, I mailed him a copy of *Recuerdos de los viejitos: Tales of the Río Puerco*, my first book on oral history published in 1987.

Manuel Alvar died in 2001. On August 15, 2001, the Madrid newspaper *El País* noted his passing with the following words, "Desaparece el gran experto de los dialectos." (The great dialect expert is gone.) He was seventy-eight years old.

Pittsburgh

An Unforeseen Place

LET US GO BACK FOR a moment to the Albaicín in Granada where Jan and I lived at Mercedes Garoffolo's Carmen while I attended the University of Granada. It was the night of December 31, 1964. A small group of us came together at her place, including two priests from the Cartuja Monastery (La Cartuja de Granada) who were invited to ring in the New Year.

As the middle of the night drew near, we all congregated around a long wooden table in the spacious living room and chatted and waited for the grandfather clock to strike twelve o'clock. About five minutes before midnight Marcelo, one of the priests, reached for a large cluster of grapes on top of the table and gave each one of us twelve grapes. "Estas son las doce uvas de la suerte." (These are the twelve grapes of luck.) In this country, as some of you know, we have a Spanish tradition. You eat the grapes to welcome the New Year. For the benefit of Nasario and Juanita (Jan) from the United States, here's what you do. As the lone church bell nearby begins to toll, you swallow a grape after each clang, one for each month of the New Year. Bueno, ¿listos? Ready?" and soon the lonesome church bell tolled its first ring. I took a grape and swallowed it, just as the priest instructed us. Then came the second and third. By now Father Marcelo noticed that I was gagging. "¡No, no Nasario! Hay que mascarlas." (You must chew them.) Everyone had a good laugh. What a cheerful way to welcome 1965. Perhaps that light moment was even a good omen as to what loomed on the Spanish horizon for me and my wife as we rang in the New Year.

Soon thereafter, as I mentioned in the previous chapter, we received a letter in early January 1965 from Jack E. Tomlin at Chatham College in Pittsburgh. The gist of his communication pertained to his starting a Portuguese program at Chatham College, a girls' private liberal arts college, but hiring someone to replace him in Spanish was of paramount importance. He thought of me as a possible replacement although he wasn't sure Pittsburgh was where Jan and I might want to settle after our return to the United States. An exchange of letters ensued between us.

On January 25 we received a follow up letter in which Tomlins said, "I can safely say that for the purposes of beginning one's teaching career, formally. . . . Chatham does offer splendid opportunities. You would be directing courses and directing senior theses and writing lectures and piddling from time to time in the language lab. As I said, 'awfully good experience, really.' I've already put in my good word with the chairman and with the dean. I don't know what weight—if any—that carries, but you can know for sure that I'll do my best for you when my opinion is asked. I've already *volunteered* it."

Given our financial state with no other options at hand, my wife and I decided to pursue the teaching position at Chatham College. Upon request from the chairman of the Language Department, I mailed my academic credentials plus names of three references. A few weeks later, February 21 to be exact, Jack Tomlins wrote us again with these promising words, "My opinion is that it looks good right now, but I still can't assure you of the outcome. It's now out of Jim's [the chairman] and my hands. So, let's hope . . ."

On March 1, I received a formal letter from President Edward Eddy who offered me the position in Spanish for the academic year 1965–1966. It read in part, "I have reviewed with Dean Henderson,

Dr. [Jim] McLaren and Dr. Tomlins the correspondence with you. Ordinarily we do not make appointment to the Chatham faculty without a personal interview on the campus. (This practice safeguards both the College *and* the individual who might also be misled.) In your case, because you are not available for an interview and because you and Dr. Tomlins are personally acquainted, we can move with greater certainty perhaps on both our parts. If you are willing to accept an appointment for teaching to begin in early September, we would be happy to have you join us in 1965–1966 as Instructor in Spanish."

My wife and I were overjoyed—and so was Jack Tomlins who wrote to us and said, "It's been many a moon since old Chatham College has hired *anybody* sight unseen; so I think you can safely say you've pulled off a *coup!*" I wrote Jack immediately to thank him.

The spring semester had begun at the University of Granada and by then I could concentrate on my graduate courses without personal finances hovering over our heads. I successfully completed the doctoral courses in late June.

We returned to Albuquerque from Europe in July 1965 to prepare for our anticipated journey to Pittsburgh. Among other things, we bought a new car, a 1965 Ford Mustang. At the beginning of August, we rented a five-by-seven-foot U-Haul trailer with all our personal possessions and embarked on our long trip, approximately 1,600 miles away that took two-and-a-half days. The trip was incredible. We traversed states, cities, and landscapes that for the most part were alien to me.

We arrived at Chatham College one early afternoon. Upon driving onto the self-contained campus, we were awestruck by the palatial mansions on the verdant and picturesque grounds. Some of the mansions, donated by wealthy barons, we learned later, were converted to dormitories. The more modern administrative building housed a potpourri of workplaces, including the president's office, faculty offices, and classrooms. The imposing chapel on top of a hill as we drove up to the administration building too was modern.

We introduced ourselves to Burt Ashman, business manager, with whom I had corresponded prior to our arrival. He had offered us—and we accepted—a third-floor efficiency apartment for seventy-five dollars per month. The Victorian house on Murray Hill Avenue belonged to the college and bordered the south side of the campus a scant five-minute walk from our apartment to my faculty office in the administration building. This was to be our home for the subsequent three years.

Established in 1869, Chatham College, today called Chatham University, is co-educational with graduate and undergraduate programs. It was an all-girls' liberal arts college until 2015, when it began enrolling men. Chatham College is situated at the hub of Squirrel Hill, the Jewish community east of the campus. West of the college is the historic Shadyside neighborhood.

Orientation for administrative personnel, staff, and faculty officially opened the academic year 1965–1966. Edward "Ted" Eddy, the president, convened the meeting followed by introduction of key top-level administrators. They in turn introduced deans and department chairmen. One by one the chairman of the Department of Languages introduced the returning faculty. I was the only new faculty member, and Jack E. Tomlins introduced me. His introductory remarks made me feel at home even though I was far from Albuquerque.

The fall semester began in earnest. I was scheduled to teach three courses: Beginning Spanish, Intermediate Spanish, and Introduction to Spanish Literature. In addition, I was to direct one or possibly two senior tutorials or theses. Except for teaching Beginning Portuguese to Peace Corps Trainees at the University of New Mexico, I was a novice in the classroom but eager to launch my long-standing career in academia.

I quickly learned there is a vast difference between being a student versus an instructor. The demands on my precious time from sunup till bedtime were incalculable. Teaching was demanding, tiresome, but rewarding and enjoyable. As the semester progressed the time devoted to the preparation of my classes did not abate. I learned very quickly, too, that there is no substitute for being a good teacher other than to know your subject matter well. I came to know also that if a student asked a question and you didn't know the answer, it behooved you to be truthful. Students are very perceptive and can detect dishonesty in your face if not in your response. They respected you more if you said, "Sorry. I don't know the answer to your query, but I'll find out and get back to you."

Unlike my experiences as a student at the University of New Mexico or in Spain, at Chatham College students adhered to a mutual code of honor. The honor system compelled them to behave with utmost integrity. At the same time they were mindful of the intellectual freedom and welfare at risk. A valued hint of the forgoing principles was brought to light the first time I scheduled an examination in one of my courses. The code of honor was invoked and honored. Students were their own best guardians.

Professors never proctored examinations or worried about cheating. I was duly impressed. As an instructor I distributed the exams, explained or clarified if necessary any aspects of the tests, and I left the classroom. I made myself available in my office in case students had any questions.

Saturdays were a day of rest and recuperation. Jan and I took romantic strolls through Chatham College's idyllic campus. The mixture of colorful autumn leaves from the assortment of trees adorned the ground. This provided an exquisite backdrop to the overall autumn scenario, a truly beautiful and secluded landscape-treasures in Pittsburgh. A colleague in the Language Department once told me, "The beauty of this campus is worth at least $1,000 on your contract." Exaggerated or not, the bucolic campus rivaled some of the more beautiful gardens in Europe that my wife and I visited. They included those in Spain and Portugal.

Being young and scarcely into the third year of our marriage helped us see nature's beauty from a different and appreciable perspective. My wife and I have fond memories of Chatham College's pastoral setting amid the mansions-turned dormitories where young ladies lived in splendor.

I was not much older than some of my students. That being so, I could relate to them easier than some of my older colleagues. Helpful as well was the fact that I had just returned from being a student at the University of Granada in Spain. Living there and traveling in Europe—including Spain and Portugal—prepared me for Pittsburgh, a multi-cultural city with proud European roots. I did struggle with some of my students' surnames whose ancestors came from Eastern Europe. Names such as Hadziewicz, Papaduick, Zajdel, and Dabrowski were dramatically different from those I was accustomed to in my native New Mexico.

The fall semester ended with a great sigh of relief, but soon the spring semester had arrived. The beginning and intermediate classes I taught were more advanced but basically a continuation of the first semester. I had some new students, especially those in Spanish 102, Survey of Spanish Literature. This course was less demanding in preparation than Spanish 101 since I was more familiar with the authors and literary movements of the eighteenth through the twentieth centuries.

Added to my spring semester schedule, I served on the Admissions Committee whose role was to peruse and evaluate applicants' academic credentials and henceforth recommend or reject admission. It was a competitive process based on GPA, SAT or ACT scores.

Letters of recommendation from high school teachers, counselors, or private citizens also comprised part of the students' dossier. One letter in support of a prospective student that I was able to read was from Hubert H. Humphrey, the former vice president under Lyndon B. Johnson.

Numerous students came from the eastern seaboard and other parts of the United States, but all of them with rare exception, I soon learned, were highly motivated and intelligent with a penchant for curiosity and learning.

During the intervening time, as I settled in my teaching job, I was accepted in the Department of Romance Languages and Literatures at the University of Pittsburgh to pursue a PhD in nineteenth-century Spanish literature. To seek a terminal degree in one's field of personal interest is something the powers that be at Chatham College advocated on behalf of junior faculty.

The spring semester of 1966 at Chatham College ended with a bit of excitement. One of the graduates was the daughter of Secretary of Defense Robert S. McNamara who served under Presidents John F. Kennedy and Lyndon B. Johnson. Not only did McNamara deliver the commencement address, but he had the honor of presenting his daughter her diploma. My first commencement exercises as a faculty member together with all of the buzz, that is, press coverage and high security required because of McNamara's stature was extraordinary and indeed a special moment.

Aside from my teaching, little did I realize that the next three years at Chatham College were to provide all sorts of wonderful memories that remain with me up till now. At the behest of students' organizations or groups and the endorsement of the dean of students, guest artists or scholars were invited to conduct workshops or deliver lectures on campus. Oftentimes actors put on performances and the entire academic community along with their families attended.

Two screen idols, Ruby Dee and Ossie Davis, husband and wife, were guests during my teaching days at Chatham College. They conducted workshops for students and performed at the non-denominational campus chapel for the entire college community to enjoy.

The renowned psychologist B. F. Skinner had taught at Chatham College before my tenure. One given summer he rented the first and second floors of the Victorian home that a colleague of mine and his spouse rented. (My wife and I lived on the third floor.) While there, Skinner conducted experiments related to his so-called Skinner's Box. He sat his infant grandchild on the terrace below our apartment as part of his empirical research. I never met Skinner, but his experiments with his grandchild needless to say pique my own interest.

Chatham College was well-known for inviting high-profile individuals such as Margaret Mead, the anthropologist, and Alan Ginsberg, the poet. I learned as well that Rachel Carson author of celebrated *Silent Spring* was a graduate of Chatham College.

Whether intellectuals, stage performers, or politicians, their presence on campus was enriching and invigorating for the entire academic community. True, the college was buffered on one side by Shadyside where you found historic homes, upscale stores, popular cafes, and restaurants. On the opposite side was Squirrel Hill, considered at that time (1960s) the hub of the Jewish community. It enjoyed a cluster of eateries, food stores and marts, drug stores and soda fountains, plus clothing outlets. Although Chatham College was seemingly isolated in its idyllic setting, the students were never out of touch with the external world.

A certain amount of intellectual reciprocity between professors from the University of Pittsburgh and Carnegie Institute of Technology—later named Carnegie Mellon University—and Chatham

College existed. Scholars from the three campuses delivered lectures that benefitted students in particular and the academic community at large.

My remaining three years (1966–1969) at Chatham College, I juggled my teaching and doctorate courses at the University of Pittsburgh, or Pitt as it is commonly referred to in local jargon (more regarding my studies at Pitt in chapter 9). In addition to the courses mentioned earlier (e.g., Beginning Spanish), I taught new classes such as the Short Story of Spanish America that required plenty of preparation since my literary interests rested in Spain, Portugal, and Brazil. I had read the works of storytellers, among them Juan Rulfo, one of my favorite authors, Jorge Luis Borges, Julio Cortázar, María Luisa Bombal, and Gabriel García Márquez who won the 1982 Nobel Prize for Literature.

Meanwhile, Dr. Albert R. Lopes, my mentor at the University of New Mexico, planned to retire. Consequently, Jack E. Tomlins applied for and was offered the position in Portuguese. He left Chatham College in 1968 to replace Dr. Lopes.

I was asked to teach Beginning Portuguese in addition to the Spanish courses. Fortunately my wife, who also has a master's in Portuguese (from the University of Wisconsin -Madison), taught the course with the blessings of the president without drafting a separate contract for my wife. His gratuitous gesture enabled me to devote more time to my doctoral studies.

My tenure at Chatham College, whether in the classroom or away from it, proved immensely enriching and gratifying. Everyone, from the president, fellow administrators, and staff to the faculty, exhibited utmost professionalism. The wholehearted support, both moral and professional, that I received—in particular from the president in my quest to finish the PhD— cannot be readily forgotten.

I tendered my resignation at Chatham College in 1969 to assume a teaching position at Northern Illinois University. The timing was ideal since I had just fulfilled all requirements toward the PhD except for the dissertation (see chapter 10).

But a capstone to the intellectual environment at Chatham College was due in large measure to the students. They were bright, highly motivated, and a joy to teach. In fact, one of my students who majored in Spanish (she was our babysitter), finished her PhD at Brown University before I was awarded mine. I have fond memories of the students at Pittsburgh's prestigious girls' private institution. What a marvelous place to have begun my thirty-six-year career in academia.

A Dream Becomes a Reality

ON MARCH 15, 1965, TWO weeks after I signed a contract with Chatham College, I wrote a letter from Granada, Spain, to Jack Kolbert, chairman of the Department of Romance Languages and Literatures at the University of Pittsburgh. I inquired whether graduate courses would be offered in Spanish language or literature during the summer. On April 1, he answered. "For the first time in more than a decade this Department does not offer summer school work for graduate students this year. . . . It seems that you would be granted full credit for work done at UNM and in Spain, leaving three semesters more of full residence study (including the dissertation) as a minimum." Kolbert was gracious enough to send me applications forms for admission into their graduate program plus a graduate catalog. In the fall, 1965, I visited the University of Pittsburgh, but Jack Kolbert was no longer there. In the interim, ironically, he had accepted a teaching position at the University of New Mexico.

From Granada I mailed my application to the University of Pittsburgh for Admission to Graduate Study. On December 1, 1965—by now I was teaching at Chatham College—I received a letter from the associate dean in which he wrote, "It is a pleasure to inform you that the Committee on Graduate Study in the Division of the Humanities admits you to full graduate status, beginning with the Winter Trimester, 1965–1966." Two years later, August 17, 1967, the dean informed me that the twelve hours of doctoral courses (*cursos monográficos*) at the University of Granada could "be applied as advanced standing toward the PhD degree with Romance Languages and Literatures as the major department of graduate study." I was elated.

Prior to the end of December 1965, I made an appointment to see Dr. Rodolfo Cardona, chairman of the Department of Romance Languages and Literatures who was assigned my academic advisor. I went to discuss my program of studies and the requisites for the PhD.

I drove to the University of Pittsburgh's academic center called Oakland. There looming majestically was the unmistakable forty-two-story Cathedral of Learning, the tallest educational building in the United States and the hub of the university campus. At first sight the Gothic style edifice was awe-inspiring and imposing. The Cathedral of Yearning, as the students dubbed it, seemed to ascend endlessly into the heavens. It was a dramatic contrast to the one-room adobe schoolhouse where I began my schooling in my native Río Puerco Valley in New Mexico. The nonsectarian Heinz Memorial Chapel, a historic landmark nearby that belongs to the university, enhanced the campus's beauty and grandeur.

Rodolfo Cardona's office was situated on the sixteenth floor of the Cathedral of Learning. I had never ridden more than five or six stories on an elevator. Cardona, professor of Spanish, was a specialist on Benito Pérez Galdós, the renowned nineteenth-century Spanish novelist. (In 1966 Cardona launched the prestigious journal *Anales Galdosianos* that published scholarly articles solely on Galdós.) For my master's thesis in Portuguese—as mentioned in chapter 6—I had compared certain religious aspects in selected works of Benito Pérez Galdós and Eça de Queiroz's *O Crime do Padre Amaro*, the celebrated nineteenth-century Portuguese novelist. Because of my genuine interest in Galdós, professor Cardona and I struck an immediate friendship. I found him to be a veritable gentleman. We discussed the department's Statement of Graduate Policy and the requirements for the PhD I could select one of three areas toward the degree: romance languages and literatures; romance linguistics; or Hispanic languages and literature. I opted to pursue the latter.

A minimum of ten, three–credit hour courses for a doctorate

in Hispanic languages and literatures was required. They included courses in one's intended field of specialization, two in Hispanic American literature, and two in linguistics. The remaining non-course requirements were outlined in the Statement of Graduate Policy: (1) a preliminary examination (2) a reading knowledge of two Romance Languages other than the major language [i.e., Spanish] (3) a comprehensive written and oral examinations (4) *explicación de texto* (5) a dissertation, and (6) a final oral examination.

A reading list was available but intended only as guide in preparation for the preliminary examination. This exam had to be successfully completed within two calendar years from the time a student first registered for graduate study if s–he wished to become a candidate for the PhD. This stipulation applied particularly to students like me who had not earned the master's at the University of Pittsburgh.

From the winter trimester, 1965–1966, until the fall trimester, 1968–1969, I enrolled in and completed nine courses (twenty-seven hours total) in different literary periods and genres in addition to linguistics, as partial fulfillment toward the doctorate. I maintained an A average in all my courses. The twelve credit hours from the University of Granada totaled thirty-nine hours.

My first course at Pitt, as students called it, taught by a visiting professor from Scotland, was a seminar on the picaresque novel, a genre I thoroughly enjoyed. From *Lazarillo de Tormes* featuring the little *pícaro* Lazarillo, *Guzmán de Alfarache* to *La vida del buscón* were works I was familiar with from my undergraduate studies at the University of New Mexico. The lesser known *El diablo cojuelo* and *La lozana andaluza* complemented the above courses.

Since it was my first class at Pitt, and not knowing how demanding the professors might be compared to those in New Mexico, I poured my heart and soul into the course. Little by little I adapted to the professor's lectures and discussions without much difficulty.

As for my classmates, two or three of whom had master's degrees from Harvard, Columbia, and the University of Pennsylvania, I was in awe. They were bright and articulate, but I rapidly realized that I could measure up to them and my other classmates. I attributed my confidence to the excellent training I received in Spanish and Portuguese at the University of New Mexico as well as my doctoral experience at the University of Granada.

Soon after the semester ended, I was anxious to find out what kind of a grade I had received for the class on the picaresque novel. The research paper comprised the main requirement for the course besides weekly reading assignments, class discussions and participation. I retrieved my paper at the language department (the professor had already returned to Scotland). A handwritten note appeared on the title page with the grade of A. It read as follows, "While the focus of your paper could have been more refined, it is well-written and clearly the product of an intelligent mind." I relished the moment, but there would be others, including surprises as well as disappointments during my graduate days at my future alma mater.

One happy moment albeit minute in the total scheme of schemes was the aptitude test in two languages other than Spanish that students were required to take. On April 8, 1967, I passed a written test in Italian (I received an A), but I was exempt from the second language since I had a master's in Portuguese.

By and large the remaining courses (1967–1969), aside from the Picaresque Novel, were enjoyable and a worthwhile learning experience. Instructors for the most part ran the gamut from exciting, good to boring but hardly ever incompetent.

Students thought that at least one instructor, Professor Alvaro (not his real name) tended to be arrogant and condescending. He was also perceived as being aloof and inclined to treating students as though he were the master and we his slaves. Some classmates were convinced that such brashness emanated from being insecure or he suffered from an inferiority complex. Others assumed he had a grudge since he was already in his mid-forties and only recently received his PhD. To further deflate his ego, he was just an assistant professor and the junior member of the department whereas his colleagues were the same age or younger, tenured, and held the rank of associate or full professor.

On November 28, 1967, strangely enough I received a formal letter from Professor Alvaro who was now acting department head. "Dear Mr. García: It is my pleasant duty to inform you that the Committee finds that you have successfully passed the preliminary examination towards the PhD degree."

My main objective at this juncture was to finish the litany of courses in preparation for the comprehensive examination. The questions were apt to cover not only the three areas of non-specialization, in my case the Middle Ages, Golden Age, and linguistics. But included as well were topics pertaining to nineteenth-century Spanish literature, my chosen field of concentration, in particular the novel.

The comprehensive examination was given in the spring of 1969 to about four or five PhD candidates. The rest, about the same number, were master's candidates. I learned soon after the exam that at least two doctoral candidates had attempted suicide. One was a classmate whom I knew. I was heartbroken, to say the least. He never returned to the university to finish his PhD. Such were the pressures that took a toll on students.

An integral part of the exam comprised fifty identifications (e.g., author, works, etc.) that encompassed movements from Medieval Spanish literature up to and including the twentieth century. Once the test was over, I became concerned because I knew the answers to only about fifteen or one-third of the fifty identifications. Some authors, titles, or sub-literary genres were esoteric at best.

Soon thereafter I saw Professor Alvaro and although he was unfriendly and not the easiest person to talk to, I broached the subject regarding the identification questions. "Oh," he explained matter-of-factly. "I drew up the list myself. You got the highest score of those who took the exam. Besides, I included some rather obscure authors and titles so I didn't expect students to know many items on the list." I found his last comment rather empty-headed and strange. I wondered silently if this was a game he played to torment students or to show his position of authority or both. I was mystified at his behavior. I had studied Golden Age drama under him and knew that he demanded a lot in terms of reading assignments, class discussions, and in-depth research papers.

On March 31, 1969, I received a letter from my advisor, Dr. Cardona, that read, "I am happy to inform you that you have passed the comprehensive examination for the PhD. I take this opportunity to congratulate you for your accomplishment." I was overjoyed at the news. Next I had to take the *explicación de texto*, the penultimate requisite prior to the dissertation. Dr. Cardona assigned me a passage from Benito Pérez Galdós's popular novel *Doña Perfecta*. My task was to explain the excerpt thematically vis-à-vis the entire novel and how it impacted Doña Perfecta, the main character.

Over a given weekend I reread *Doña Perfecta* (I had read it several times) before I met with a department committee of Dr. Cardona and two faculty members. One was Professor Godoy (pseudonym) with whom I had studied Spanish American Literature; the second one was the Spaniard, Assistant Professor Alvaro, who prepared the fifty "dubious" identification questions alluded to above.

My presentation as regards the textual analysis lasted only about a half an hour after an unexpected confrontation erupted. Professor Godoy asked one or two questions and complimented me on my responses. Then it was Professor Alvaro's turn. "Please explain to me the concept of irony in the character Doña Perfecta," and I did, to which he reacted rather impetuously. "Nooooo, no, no . . ." he bellowed, but before he could finish his outburst, Professor Godoy intervened. "¿Cómo que no? Nasario ha hecho buen trabajo." (What do you mean no? Nasario did a good job.) He shouted and struck the top of the coffee table with his right fist. The empty coffee pot flew high into the air and miraculously landed upright back on the table. A dead silence ensued. Dr. Cardona was stunned. I myself could not believe the provocative and bizarre scene, but I was overjoyed that the full professor had come to my defense. "Nasario, please step outside for a moment," Dr. Cardona requested.

No more than five minutes elapsed at which point Professor Alvaro emerged from the seminar room. "¡Felicidades! Congratulations!" he said. "You've passed your *explicación de texto.*" I felt then, as I do to this day, that he was told to congratulate me as a means of offering his apologies or perhaps as a way of humiliating him for his impulsive outburst. There was an obvious dislike between him, an assistant professor, and the Latin American professor who outranked him.

The road heretofore in pursuit of my doctorate while juggling my time between teaching full-time at Chatham College and taking classes had been tiring and a challenge. Now only the dissertation and oral defense remained. A glimmer of hope shined at the end of the proverbial tunnel, but alas soon afterward Dr. Cardona my dissertation director informed me that he had accepted a position in Texas. Instead of my choosing a new director as stipulated in the language department's Statement of Graduate Policy, he told me that Professor Alvaro would direct my dissertation. Purportedly, there was no one else in the department with expertise in nineteenth-century Spanish literature, my chosen area of specialization. I accepted the glum news with mixed emotions and trepidation.

Never in my life did I envision that working with that man would turn into a veritable nightmare and gut-wrenching experience, but first things first. There was a series of bureaucratic steps that had to be undertaken before a student could actually begin to do research and start organizing and writing the dissertation.

I met with Professor Alvaro to discuss a topic and settled on "Religiosity in the Novels of Benito Pérez Galdós." I then filed an application with the Graduate Office of Arts and Sciences to be admitted to the candidacy for the degree of Doctor of Philosophy. I officially became a candidate on June 16, 1969. Thereafter I had to request for the Graduate Office to forward the pertinent documents to my dissertation director in order to establish a dissertation committee for the oral defense. Said committee of no fewer than four members, including one from a department outside languages, was apt to change later.

In early fall of 1969, I mailed to Professor Alvaro the five-page prospectus titled "Religiosity in the Novels of Benito Pérez Galdós." This title later changed to "Religious Equivocation in the Novels of Benito Pérez Galdós." I did not receive an acknowledgment. By now I was teaching at Northern Illinois University in DeKalb, Illinois (more in chapter 10).

As the semester progressed I sent him a copy of chapters 1, 2, and 3. Once again I asked him to acknowledge receipt of my work. After several weeks of no response, I wrote to him to inquire on the status of my prospectus, the introduction, and two additional chapters, but he still failed to respond. In January 1971 (two-plus years later!), I finally heard from him with copious editorial notes criticizing my writing style and challenging several of my interpretative analysis.

His patronizing comments were a prelude to the arduous work and frustration that lay ahead for me. It is difficult to proclaim many years later whether such behavior was symptomatic of forgetfulness, indifference, arrogance, or incompetence. I even entertained the notion of revenge on his part for getting berated by his colleague at the *explicación de texto*.

I wrote and rewrote chapters 2 and 3 numerous times. Each time I inserted his editing and corrections but then waited forever for him to return the corrected chapters with his final approval before I proceeded to the next chapter. After a careful reading I discovered that by now he was correcting his own previous suggestions and editorial changes. He did this time and again. It was the classic story of the tail wagging the dog. To say that it was frustrating and nerve-wrenching would be an understatement. Whatever problems bedeviled him, I had too much at stake in terms of time, effort, and frustrations, not to mention thousands of dollars invested in tuition, to yield to his personal whims.

The tug of war, as it were, lasted from the time I was admitted to the candidacy for the PhD in June 1969 until the fall semester of 1972. By then the statute of limitations to finish the dissertation had expired, and I had to petition the Graduate Office for an extension.

Then, much to my astonishment, I received a telephone call in early October 1972 from Professor Alvaro. I was shocked to learn that he was now teaching at another university outside Pennsylvania. He was straight and to the point, "Send me a complete set of your dissertation. We need to wrap things up." Fortunately, despite his incessant inattentiveness and procrastination of three-plus years, in the interim I had the presence of mind to write the remaining four chapters. Almost immediately I sent him a complete draft of my dissertation, seven chapters total.

On October 16, 1972, I received in the mail a brief note from him that read as follows, "This is merely to let you know that your thesis arrived today. I'll get to work on it and get back to you as soon as I can." Thereafter he proceeded rather expeditiously. He offered a few suggestions and corrections, but this time unlike in the past he did not dwell on minutiae or correct his own editing. A preliminary approval of the dissertation occurred about mid-November at which time I made copies for him and members of the orals' committee as per procedure. An oral defense was scheduled for December 5, 1972, on campus at the Cathedral of Learning.

I drove from Illinois to Pittsburgh and met with Professor Alvaro and the orals' committee. The guests on the committee had impeccable credentials. The two professors of Spanish had doctorate degrees from the Universidad Complutense de Madrid and Harvard University, respectively. The outside member came from the English Department and possessed a PhD from Columbia University.

The oral defense went smoothly. I presented a brief introduction on the novelist Benito Pérez Galdós and a synopsis regarding religious equivocation in selected novels, the central focus of my dissertation. The guests were cordial, respectful, and professional. They asked a few questions and suggested several editorial changes that I incorporated into the dissertation.

A copy was prepared, approved by my director, and submitted to the Graduate Office. Final approval of my dissertation is dated December 11, 1972, with December 20, 1972, as the official date of having received my PhD. My diploma, postmarked May 10, 1973, was mailed to me in DeKalb, Illinois, where I had been teaching for the past three years at Northern Illinois University (NIU). Coincidentally my diploma was cosigned by Rhoten A. Smith, the former president of NIU. He now held the position of provost at the University of Pittsburgh.

With PhD in hand, I breathed a huge sigh of relief after being in limbo since I passed my comprehensive examinations on May 14, 1969. In retrospect, my dissertation director's failure to honor his responsibility to students was insensitive and inhumane. Upon his departure from the University of Pittsburgh he did not have the professional courtesy to notify either me or two other students (one of them my friend) who were writing their dissertation under his guidance. Some benevolent individual in the administrative hierarchy, perhaps the department head or dean, came to our rescue and doubtless impressed upon him to fulfill his professional and educational obligation to his students.

I had vowed to fly my parents to Pittsburgh so they could join my wife and me in the graduation ceremonies, but regrettably my mother passed away on May 25, 1972 seventeen years to the day after I graduated from high school—at the young age of fifty-two. In deference to her, I cancelled all plans to attend commencement exercises.

Now in honor of my beloved parents I was prepared to devote my career to academia forever mindful that my father* quit the fifth grade to help his parents on the farm. My mother, on the other hand, never attended a day of school.†

---

* My father, a widower and an octogenarian, watched *Sesame Street*; he hoped to improve what little English he knew in order to listen to the local and national news. "If a bird (i.e., Big Bird) can speak English," he once told me with a wry smile, "so can I."

† During the 1950s Mom, in her late thirties and a mother of eight children, discovered *Queen for A Day*, a television program that featured poor women. She was inspired to learn bits and pieces of English. Whenever the Raleigh Man came around selling his products to housewives in the neighborhood, she was thrilled to converse at a basic level with him. I was proud of her.

Amid Del Monte Cornfields

IN THE SPRING OF 1969 a former graduate student I knew at the University of New Mexico wrote to me at Chatham College in Pittsburgh. He was chairman of the Department of Languages at Northern Illinois University in DeKalb, Illinois, located about fifty miles west of Chicago. He asked if I would be interested in a teaching position. I went for an interview and was offered a position as an assistant professor of Spanish, which I accepted. This was an opportunity to move west though still far from New Mexico my ultimate destination provided everything panned out professionally.

My wife, our two-year old daughter Michele who was born in Pittsburgh, and I moved to DeKalb, Illinois, in late July 1969. Northern Illinois University (NIU) was a dramatic contrast to Chatham College's student body of 650 female students whereas NIU was coeducational and boasted upwards of 20,000 students and more than 1,000 faculty members. The Department of Foreign Languages alone had over forty instructors compared to my eight colleagues at Chatham College.

The department head who hired me at NIU, much to my surprise and chagrin, was no longer there when I attended my first departmental meeting at the start of the fall semester. I felt like a total stranger in a sea of new colleagues.

To make matters worse, as recounted in the previous chapter, I never envisioned how the dissertation would hover over me like a perpetual black halo for three seemingly endless years. One person who helped alleviate the pressure was Dorothy Allen the new department head. She was gracious enough to offer me a light teaching schedule conducive to writing the dissertation. I taught three fresh-men and sophomore classes that did not require an inordinate amount of preparation, but I never short-changed my students. They were a top-priority in my new position and throughout my teaching career.

One given year at Professor Allen's behest I taught only two courses. But in lieu of the third class I visited and evaluated student teachers at high schools or middle schools in the region. The schools had reciprocal agreements with NIU's Department of Education and the Department of Foreign Languages regarding prospective teachers. I visited aspiring teachers in places like Rockford, Cicero, a multiethnic and blue-collar community west of Chicago and the Jack Benny Middle School in northern Chicago named in honor of the comedian a Chicago native.

My tenure at NIU was not flamboyant, but I'm pleased to say that the most rewarding experience occurred one hour away at the Illinois State Penitentiary in Joliet (Stateville). There under the aus-pices of the Extension College Program I taught inmates Beginning Spanish I and II during AY 1972–1973.

My first trip to the prison was eerie and unlike anything I had experienced in my teaching years. I arrived and parked the univer-sity car outside the penitentiary and proceeded to secure clearance from the security guard at the main entrance. I signed in, jotted the time and purpose of my visit, as well as to leave all of my personal effects (e.g., billfold, car keys) in a plastic bag with my name printed on it. The guard then gave me a name tag to pin on the lapel of my sport's jacket. The security measures thereafter until I reached the cellblocks were an eye opener. A guard escorted me through numer-ous electrically clanging operated iron gates. As we stopped at each checkpoint, I had to state my name and purpose of visit while the respective guard in charge eyed my nametag.

The stern and not very talkative guard accompanied me to the cellblock that housed the educational classrooms. He introduced me to Harley M. Kuriger, the director of the Extension College Program, and departed. After the cordial director extended his personal greetings, he ushered me to the classroom.

"I want you to meet Professor García. He'll be your instructor of Spanish for the fall semester. He comes from Northern. Please give him a warm welcome," and the inmates applauded as the director departed.

"Thank you. Thank you for your nice reception," I responded. "This is the first time I've taught at Statesville. I'm really looking forward to the semester," and I glanced at the dozen or so students. The first thing that attracted my attention was their neatly ironed attire. They resembled clones since they were all dressed in blue pants and shirts with their surname in white letters above the left-hand shirt pocket reminiscent of my army days.

"I have a class list that the director gave me with your names on it. I will read each name out loud to make sure your own name is on the list. Please respond *aquí*, here, if I call your name. If I don't state your name, don't say anything," and they all chuckled. I knew at that instant that I was going to enjoy the class.

As I read the names, Joe Green, David Hill, Clarence McWilliams, Ray Scott, José Rodríguez, etc. (not their real names), they mirrored those of my students on campus with one noticeable exception. The first names of course were all male. Another thing that I noticed on the roster was the fact that the inmates all had the same PO Box number and zip code. These were but two anomalies that I encountered at the penitentiary.

Every Tuesday for the rest of the semester I checked out a university car from the motor pool and drove to the prison. The one-hour drive via green flatlands and farms was monotonous. Little by little I became accustomed to the "check in and checkout" routine at the penal institution in addition to other security measures. The clanging of iron gates in the main building before I exited and entered the prison yard en route to my classroom in Cellblock D were rueful reminders of an oppressive environment. Midway through the semester I was permitted to leave the guardhouse, enter the prison, and proceed to my class minus an escort.

As time elapsed I adapted to the rigid institutional rules visitors had to abide by. On the other hand, regimentation for those of us who taught at the prison had its own redeeming rewards. Students in my Spanish I and II without fail came to class well-prepared and were eager to participate in oral class responses and anxious to learn. Then again, it behooved them to earn good grades that were recorded on their academic dossier. The administration and the Parole Board looked favorably on academic achievement whenever inmates appeared before the Parole Board for release from prison.

The final course that I taught at the prison was Intermediate Spanish Conversation. That was during the summer of 1973. Several of the students were from my Beginning Spanish classes. By the end of the course, most of them were fairly conversant in Spanish, but one topic deemed taboo in class discussions was the reason for their incarceration. Anything else was "fair game" (the inmates' words). One thing I overhead from their rumblings during the fifteen-minute breaks of our three-hour class was the fact that they all considered themselves innocent victims of a rigged and biased justice system. Their crimes ran the gamut from domestic violence, attempted murder, or robbery to petty crimes.

Toward the end of the Summer Session, I informed the class that we would have an overall review the week before the final examination. As soon as the last word glided from the tip of my tongue an inmate stood up. "Instead of a review, could you teach us some cuss words and obscene phrases in Spanish?"

"Yeah, yeah!" echoed the entire class with one or two students applauding. "Yeah, we're tired of Pepe's *coño* (pussy) and his *pinga* (cock)," (common words among Cubans) blurted another student.

"I'll tell you what I can do. After we finish the review that will take the first half of the class period, I'll share with you a list of bad words. How's that?" "¡Arriba! ¡Arriba!" shouted Pedro the Mexican American.

The following week, unlike previous visits to the Illinois State Penitentiary (aka Joliet Prison), a guard was unexpectedly waiting to escort me to class. "What's up?" I asked. "I don't know. My supervisor asked me to take you to your classroom."

Before entering the front building to the prison and thereafter, we navigated our way through the usual clanging of iron gates. At that instant I saw a group of guards leaving the main building with an inmate in shackles. I learned later that he was Richard Speck the notorious killer of a dozen-plus nurses in a Chicago hospital. They were taking him to a hospital in Cook County for treatment of an undisclosed illness.

On the other hand, the Joliet Prison became famous because of a scene in "The Blues Brothers," the 1980 comedy starring Dan Aykroyd and the late John Belushi.

When the guard and I arrived at the classroom, inmates besides my students were practically hanging from the rafters. I walked in amid applause that surprised me. Then Gabe Dillon (not his real name) stood up and spoke.

"Dr. García, first of all, my classmates and I want to thank you for coming to teach the class this summer. However, the director has told us that you won't be coming back in the fall 'cause you're moving to Colorado. Is that right?"

"That's right. My wife, daughters Michele and Raquel, who was born in DeKalb, and I are moving to Pueblo, Colorado, to be closer to our families in Albuquerque. I have accepted a teaching position at Southern Colorado State College (SCSC)." Dead silence ensued.

"Oh, I forgot to mention," interjected Dillon, breaking the stillness. "We have some visitors. The director said it was okay. They're from our cellblock and are here to learn the cuss words you're going to teach us." Applause.

While I reviewed the relevant material for the final examination, the visiting inmates sat quietly although some did their share of fidgeting. They were anxious no doubt to hear the profane language I was about to share with them and the students in my class. After a short break, I said, "Okay, get your pens and pencils ready. Here's what you've been waiting for," and everyone hooped and hollered. I wrote in huge letters on the blackboard LEXICUM VULGARUM. As soon as I jotted down these words I heard a chorus of "What? What the f- - -!" I began writing in random order a series of nasty words and phrases common among Hispanics in New Mexico and southern Colorado. Not one inmate wasted time in feverishly copying the words from the blackboard.

The week of the final examination was rather perfunctory except for a security guard who once again waited at the main gate to accompany me to the classroom. Before I could ask him why I was being escorted, he said to me. "Sir, what did you do to those students of yours?" "Why?" I asked. "Because all week long they've been using strange words that we believe are code words. We think they're planning a coup or something."

I chuckled since I knew what prompted his comments. The inmates obviously had fun throughout the week using the salacious language. I had cautioned everyone to be careful in the use of the vulgar terms lest they get into trouble or have their teeth knocked out.

I discussed final grades. Virtually all the inmates received an A or a B. One or two got Cs, but there were no Ds or Fs. I was very pleased but not surprised. After I met with each student individually, I prepared to say goodbye. At that instant, Dillon, the spokesman for the group, walked in with a large beautifully decorated cake.

"Dr. García, this cake is in your honor," he said. "We want to thank you for coming to teach us Spanish, especially the cuss words." Laughter erupted. We sat, ate cake, and drank coffee and fruit punch before I bid everyone adiós.

Soon thereafter a letter arrived in the mail; it was an invitation to the commencement exercises at the prison. My wife and I and two other Northern Illinois University colleagues attended the ceremonies. On the list of graduates were a number of my students who received their Associate of Arts (AA) degree.

Later a letter came to me dated June 30, 1973, from one of the students at the penitentiary. The spirit of the communication underscored how appreciative inmates were to have professors like me teach courses that led to their AA degrees and ultimately perchance their freedom.

Three weeks afterward, July 23, the director of the Extension College Program wrote me a glowing and gratifying letter expressing his personal appreciation.

Except for these inspiring letters, plus my erstwhile students on campus and the joy of me and my wife becoming parents for the second time (our daughter Raquel as mentioned earlier was born in DeKalb, Illinois), my tenure at Northern Illinois University was rather stressful. For more than three prolonged years, 1969–1972, the foreboding dissertation hovered over me like a perpetual dark cloud. The classroom became my therapy and the benevolent students my steadfast supporters. They were the flame that kept my heart aglow throughout the dissertation ordeal until that fateful day when I was awarded my PhD in December 1972.

By then my wife and I were eager to relocate to the West and just as anxious to leave DeKalb, Illinois, where the verdant Del Monte cornfields brimmed with pride in spring and summer; where the frigid winters with subzero temperatures and blistery winds pierced your heart and soul; and, where barbed wire was born and became eminently important—or a curse—to the rancher-farmer in western states like New Mexico and Colorado.

Pleasant Memories Linger

WITH PHD IN HAND, I applied for a faculty position at Southern Colorado State College (SCSC) in Pueblo, Colorado (first and only time in my academic career that I applied for a job of my own accord) and was invited for an interview in March 1973. I flew from O'Hare Airport in Chicago to Denver and from here I boarded a small plane to Pueblo. As we landed east of the city I could see the llano, the plains reminiscent of the Llano Estacado in eastern New Mexico.

On campus I met individually first with the president, then the vice president of academic and student affairs, thereafter the dean of Arts and Sciences, and lastly the language faculty. I was duly impressed with all of them, especially the president. He, the vice president, the dean, and I lunched at the local Country Club. Their cordial reception made me feel at home.

In early April 1973 I received a contract from the president who offered me a position as associate professor of foreign languages. (No one else in the language department possessed a PhD.) Overjoyed, I returned without hesitation a signed copy on April 10. My wife and I were eager to relocate to the West albeit in an unfamiliar place called Pueblo (or *Pieblo*, as some locals pronounce it). Southern Colorado State College and Pueblo enjoyed strong cultural and linguistic ties to Hispanics of northern New Mexico and southern Colorado (e.g., San Luis Valley).

The campus was situated northeast of the city where the six-story library loomed proudly as viewed from afar. Unbeknownst to me, my office was to be on the sixth floor of the library that bore no identifiable name. All the buildings were relatively new and featured an ultra-modern architectural design. A breathtaking view of the Rocky Mountains (Cuernos Verdes/Greenhorn Mountains toward the south and Pikes Peak in the north) dotted the mountain range west of the campus across the Fountain Creek. The stark blue skies reminiscent of New Mexico complemented the beautiful landscape.

Next to the unforgettable and enriching teaching days at Chatham College in Pittsburgh, I was on the cusp of embarking on the most exciting and rewarding period of my entire academic career. Those pleasant memories at Southern Colorado State College lurk in my mind to this day.

But first it is worth noting that Pueblo in the early 1970s, although much smaller in size and population than Pittsburgh, in a variety of ways bore a striking resemblance. Both cities relied heavily on the steel industry, that is, Jones and Laughlin (J & L Steel) in Pittsburgh, and Pueblo with its own familiar sight the Colorado Fuel and Iron Company (CF & I).

From a historical perspective Pittsburgh's vibrant multiethnic neighborhoods dot the city. Among them are East Allegheny and Mount Washington (Germans), Bloomfield (Italians), the South Side (Lithuanians), the Hill District (African American), and Squirrel Hill (Jewish).

Pueblo's multicultural mosaic mirrored that of Pittsburgh. Excepting the Denver metropolitan area, Pueblo is unique among Colorado cities. It consists of Italians, Germans, English, Irish, Slovenians, Russians, Lithuanians, and Hispanics. Each group singularly and collectively has had a remarkable impact on the proud city's history.

For me as professor of Spanish language and literatures Pueblo's cultural montage came alive in the halls and classrooms at Southern Colorado State College. The Department of Foreign Languages though small (nine faculty members) it offered majors in Spanish, French, German, and Russian.

Uppermost in my mind as I began my career at what later (July 1975) became the University of Southern Colorado was to become a top-quality teacher. Because of said commitment, I devoted the preponderance of my energies toward the preparation of classes not only to share my knowledge of language and literature but also to challenge students intellectually. Many of them were Hispanics who arrived on campus plagued with similar educational inadequacies in English reminiscent of my freshman days many years earlier at the University of New Mexico. On the other hand, they were proud, attentive, and eager to learn.

For many students their ancestral roots rested in small communities of northern New Mexico, namely, Tierra Amarilla, Chama, Peñasco, and Costilla. Others came from places in southern Colorado such as Trinidad, Walsenburg (once known as La Plaza de Los Leones), Monte Vista, Del Norte, Aguilar, García, and San Luis, the oldest town in the state founded on April 9, 1851.

Bit by bit I became acclimated to my new institution. In 1976, three years after I joined the faculty at the University of Southern Colorado (USC), I found a letter in my campus mailbox from the president of the Colorado Student National Education Association (SNEA). She informed me that I had been nominated by the student body as Educator of the Year. This award was given yearly to an outstanding educator on campus. I was humbled by the students' kind gesture.

Numerous times during my years at USC (1973–1986) I was recognized for my teaching excellence, scholarship, and/or service to the university. In the spring semester of 1978 the president wrote to me. "It is my pleasure to inform you that you have been selected an outstanding faculty member of the 1977–1978 year and will be recognized at commencement, Saturday, May 20, 1978. The selection process evaluates outstanding performance and service to USC. You are to be commended for your selection."

In 1981 I was nominated by my department, with an endorsement from the dean of the School of Liberal Arts, for exceptional contribution to the institution. The dean wrote: "During the current academic year Dr. García has coauthored a book and published three review articles, in addition to presenting papers at several national committees (conferences) and at the state level. He is a rigorous and demanding professor, highly respected by his students, and his classroom presentations are well organized and prepared with the needs of the students in mind without sacrificing academic standards. Dr. García embodies the university ideal of combined research and teaching and is therefore nominated by the School for its Outstanding Faculty Award for 1981–1982."

The heartwarming words were underscored in a letter from the vice president of academic affairs. "It is my pleasure to invite you and your spouse to the Outstanding Faculty Awards dinner . . . Monday, May 10, at 6:30 p.m. . . . I congratulate you warmly on being selected as an Outstanding Faculty member for 1981–1982. The president and the Deans and I look forward to congratulating you personally on May 10." These awards became known as the Owl Awards. The faculty member's name was inscribed on a bronze plaque. Several such honors of which I am eminently proud comprise part of my teaching memorabilia at the University of Southern Colorado.

Yet while teaching was the high point of my academic career, I was forever cognizant that scholarship and community services were pivotal as well in the overall criteria for tenure and promotion to full professor. I was awarded both in 1979–1980, six years after I joined the faculty ranks.

In April 1974 before I finished my first year at Southern Colorado State College, I received a letter from the Department of Administration in Denver. It read in part, "As a result of the Grand Jury Report regarding the Colorado State Penitentiary, Governor John D. Vanderhoof has established the following Task Forces: Health,

Education, and Administration . . . we would like to request that you become a member of the Task Force on Education to aid them in their assigned task." My teaching experience at the Illinois State Penitentiary in Joliet (see chapter 10) without doubt led to my appointment to the governor's task force.

Soon thereafter a communication came from the president of the university in which he stated: "Dear Dr. García. Please accept my congratulations upon being named to the Governor's Task Force on Education . . . I would also like . . . to congratulate you for the fine feature article in the *Pueblo Chieftain-Star Journal*. It is this type of publicity that assists in promoting Southern Colorado State College and informs the public of our community service."

As a member of the task force, we visited a number of penal and correctional facilities throughout Colorado. Our primary task was to assess their educational programs and to make recommendations to the governor and his staff on how to improve curricular offerings for inmates at the respective institutions.

In 1975 F. Kenneth Komoski, executive director, Educational Products Information Exchange Institute (EPIE) in New York City wrote me a letter. He informed me that Gary Keller, Editor, Bilingual Review, had nominated me to serve on EPIE's National Task Force on the analysis of bilingual instructional materials. A group of thirty-nine analysts from across the country met at Ghost Ranch in Abiquiú, New Mexico from September 11–19 to evaluate materials helpful toward advancing bilingual education in this country.

A few years later I was delighted to be appointed to the Colorado Commission on Libraries. This led to my being nominated by the assistant commissioner in 1979 as a delegate at large to the White House Conference on Libraries and Information Services. Letters supporting my nomination came from individuals and organizations. Included among them were United States Senator Gary Hart, the League of Women Voters, and Bev Moore, the director of the library at the University of Southern Colorado. Due to their generous support I was selected to represent Colorado at the White House Conference on Libraries in Washington, DC.

Shortly thereafter I received a letter from United States Senator Claiborne Pell, democrat, Rhode Island, and William Ford, democrat, Michigan, member, US Congress, both of whom were co-chairmen of the Subcommittee on Education. They invited me to testify before the committee, an honor indeed.

Other notables on the committee were Senators Ted Kennedy from Massachusetts, Jacob Javits, New York, and John Brademas from Indiana. For me personally this was indeed one of the highlights of the conference.

My presentation before the committee focused on illiteracy in general and my immediate family in particular. I cited my paternal grandparents and my own parents who due to being poor never had the wherewithal to pursue an education in New Mexico. Neither of my grandparents ever attended school. My father, the youngest of six siblings, fared a tad better, but still he was a fifth-grade dropout. He left school to help his parents work the farmland for survival. My mother, on the other hand, never attended a day of school.

A portion of my testimony (a tape recording is in my personal archives) before the Pell-Ford Committee appeared the following day, November 20, 1979, in the *Washington Star* (1852–1981), a forerunner to the *Washington Post*. The article written by Boris Weintraub reads as follows: "One witness, Nasario García, a professor at the University of (Southern) Colorado at Pueblo, spoke movingly of the need to establish programs to fight illiteracy, which is a condition of life for an estimated 20 per cent of the American population. 'My father is the ninth generation of our family to live in this country, in New Mexico, and I am the tenth . . . I am very proud of that. But he is 67 and he cannot read or write. I urge that something be done to change this condition."

Another special moment at the White House Conference on Libraries occurred when President Jimmy Carter greeted all of the conferees. I received, as did the rest of the attendees, an invitation that read, "The President invites you to be an official participant in The White House Conference on Library and Information Services to be held November 15–November 19, 1979, Washington Hilton Hotel, Washington, D.C."

While at USC I served on a number of national, regional, state, and local organizations as part of my community service. Among professional groups I was a member of the American Association of Teachers of Spanish and Portuguese (AATSP) with chapters in the United States and abroad.

Closer to home I belonged to the Rocky Mountain Modern Language Association (RMMLA) and in 1977–1978 served as Secretary for the Symposium on Ethnic Studies. Furthermore, I was elected to the board of the Colorado Congress of Foreign Language Teachers (CCFLT). In 1982 this organization awarded me the Scholarship Award "presented to a foreign language educator who has contributed to the foreign language profession through published works or material developments."

Not to be forgotten, and to an extent of particular notable importance, is the American Issues Forum (AIF) sponsored by the Colorado State Library System, 1975–1976. The AIF embraced a series of discussions on public issues spearheaded by the faculty of the Humanities and Behavioral and Social Sciences Division at the University of Southern Colorado. The lectures celebrated the Bicentennial. My topic "Growing up in America: A Sense of Belonging" enabled me to travel to rural libraries in southern Colorado, among them Carnegie Public Library in Lamar, Florence Public Library, Rocky Ford Public Library, and Buena Vista Public Library. Here is a synopsis of my presentation:

> To be born and reared in this country denotes that a degree of loyal patriotism exists in every one of us. By extension, there is a feeling of truly belonging to America. However, most Americans would be dismayed to learn that such an outlook is nothing more than a myth—which is tantamount to self-delusion—because one, as an individual, fabricates a world (knowingly or unknowingly) within AMERICA and deduces from it, that we really belong to America. While patriotism and growing up in American may go hand-in-hand, growing up in America and feeling that you are part of America are often mutually exclusive. The question is not whether you feel that you belong to America or that America belongs to you but rather, "Does America make you feel wanted?".

My role in the American Issues Forum enabled me to reflect on my future scholarly endeavors. An area that attracted widespread attention in the early 1970s was Chicano literature. Among the better-known writers of that epoch (two or three became good friends of mine), are Tomás Rivera, Rolando Hinojosa Smith, Estella Portillo Trambley, Luis Valdez, Miguel Méndez, Ron Arias, Rudolfo Anaya, and Rodolfo "Corky" Gonzales. Last but not least there was my *paisano*, compatriot Sabine Reyes Ulibarrí whose short stories pay tribute to Hispanics of northern New Mexico. Today the foregoing writers read like a who's who in the annals of Chicano literature.

In 1974 the late Felipe Ortego (1926–2018) and David Conde arranged the First National Symposium on Chicano Literature and Critical Analysis. Held in November at New Mexico Highlands University in Las Vegas the symposium attracted more than two hundred participants from colleges and universities across the country.

Some scholars and readers included Tino Villanueva, Carlota Cárdenas, Ricardo Sánchez, Juan Bruce Novoa, and yours truly. The critical works and poetry readings underscored the blossoming of the Chicano experience. Featured were the works of pioneer authors such as Rolando Hinojosa Smith, Tomás Rivera, Ricardo Sánchez, and Luis Valdez. My presentation, titled "Satire: Techniques and Devices in Luis Valdez' *Las dos caras del patroncito* '" (The Two Faces of the Little Boss) that brought to light the evils of duplicity, not what is good or moral. My paper and a host of other studies compiled by Felipe Ortego and David Conde were published March 1975 in a volume titled *The Chicano Literary World—1974*.

Subsequent scholarly works of mine likewise were published in anthologies such as *Contemporary Chicano Fiction: A Critical Survey* and *Chicano Literature: A Reference Guide* edited by Julio A. Martínez and Francisco Lomelí. For this last work I authored an article on Anthony Rudolph Oaxaca Quinn, the renowned movie actor. My critique was based partly on his autobiography, *The Original Sin: A Self-Portrait*.

But beyond articles, my poetry, literary reviews, interviews, and essays pertaining to Chicano literature were featured in journals such as Hispania, De Colores, the *Bilingual Review-Revista Bilingüe*, *Confluencia*, and *Revista Chicano-Riqueña*.

What's more, I presented research papers at a number of conferences on Chicano literature. Among the topics discussed were "Temas, fuentes, y el futuro de la literatura chicana," "The Concept of Time in *Nambé—Year One*," based on Orlando Romero's novel, and "Chicano Bibliography for Chicano Studies Programs." In addition, I served as a panelist on "Urban Land Use" at the National Association of Chicano Studies (NACS) hosted by Colorado College, 1979.

Under the rubric Hispanic Link Symposium a group of us faculty at the University of Southern Colorado with financial support from the administration organized conferences on Chicano literature. Once a year at least two well-known authors were invited to share facets of their writings with the academic community. Our guests included: Rolando Hinojosa-Smith, *Estampas del valle*; Sabine R. Ulibarrí, *Tierra Amarilla: Stories of New Mexico–Cuentos de Nuevo México*; Ron Arias, *The Road to Tamazunchale*; and, José Antonio Burciaga, artist and poet from El Paso who became a close friend.

Within time it became patently clear that Chicano literature was a viable literary genre among critics, writers, and readers alike. Yet, I yearned for something more robust and akin to my ancestral roots that date back several centuries in New Mexico.

In June 1976 the Sangre de Cristo Arts and Conference Center in Pueblo, Colorado, hosted the Asociación Nacional de Grupos Folklóricos' third annual conference. One of the organizers was Lorenzo Trujillo, an accomplished dancer. Soon after the conference, he and I published *Festival Folklórico Mexicano: 1976*. This work is a compendium of dances, costumes, and music related to Oaxaca, Jalisco, Michoacán, Veracruz, and the American Southwest that were highlighted at the conference.

Three years later, 1979, at the behest of the Colorado Humanities Council I participated in an oral history project titled "Huérfano County Ethno-History Project." The director was Elaine Baker from Ft. Garland, Colorado. My role was to review, analyze, interpret, and evaluate more than fifty oral history interviews conducted and transcribed by community people literate in Spanish. Two articles of mine titled "Hispanos Prominent in Early Huérfano County History," and "Hispano Folklore Traced to Spain" appeared in the Huérfano World News in May 1980.

An extensive article summarizing the Hispano's contributions in the region was published afterward in the Huérfano County News. An edited version of this same article was issued years later (no date cited) by Karen Mitchell under the heading "Huérfano County, Colorado: Oral Interviews."

My participation in the Huérfano County project of Walsenburg, together with my involvement in the Pueblo conference related to Mexican folklore dances mentioned above, proved central to my personal and future interests in oral history and folklore. Combined, both were a prelude to my thirty-plus years of interviewing Hispanic old-timers of New Mexico and the American Southwest.

Said battery of Spanish interviews began in earnest in 1977 although my first tape-recorded interview—reel to reel—occurred in 1968 with my paternal grandparents. This was three years after my return from a year of doctoral work at the University of Granada in Spain. The informative question and answer exchange took place at their home in Albuquerque's Martíneztown. I explored their childhood and adult lives in the Río Puerco Valley of New Mexico southeast of Chaco Canyon where I myself spent the formative years of my life.

The informal exchange with my elderly grandparents (he was ninety-six, and she was about eighty-seven) inspired me thereafter to carve out a niche in oral history and folklore. The decision proved fortuitous since there was an abundance of scholars in nineteenth-century Spanish literature, the area of concentration for my PhD from the University of Pittsburgh.

Chicano literature alluded to earlier in this chapter was promising, but my inclination was to devote my time and energy to an area or areas more analogous to my family roots that transcend several centuries in northern New Mexico.

In the spring of 1979, I applied for a research grant at Emory University in Atlanta, Georgia to undertake a project titled "Interviews with Former Hispanic Old-Timers of the Río Puerco Valley of New Mexico." The grant, under the auspices of The Southern Fellowships Fund in Atlanta, was approved for the academic year 1980–1981. Therein rests the genesis to a multiplicity of interviews with Spanish-speaking old-timers born in New Mexico. (I was also the beneficiary of countless mini-grants at the University of Southern Colorado and New Mexico Highlands University to pursue my oral history/folklore projects.)

The academic year proved to be a banner year. In addition to the Emory University grant, I was awarded tenure as well as promoted to full professor. At this stage in my academic career I felt a certain relief and freedom in being able to engage in oral history and folklore as a practical, judicious, and worthwhile endeavor. Though I was a novice in both areas and lacked empirical knowledge vis-à-vis interviewing techniques, coalescing and assimilating materials, I was intimately familiar with Hispanic life in rural New Mexico.

From fiestas and celebrations, both secular and religious, politics, education, witchcraft and the supernatural to farming and ranching, I knew what types of questions to ask my informants, an invaluable asset to be sure. An added advantage is the fact that I personally knew many of the *viejitos*, old-timers of the Río Puerco Valley where I grew up. They were, in essence, my avowed trailblazers that culminated in thirty-plus years of interviewing Hispanic elders both in my valley and elsewhere in New Mexico and the American Southwest.

In the process I learned certain fine points in the art of interviewing. For instance, never interview husband and wife together unless you wish to play the role of mediator in case of a disagreement between them over an answer to a particular question. In some cases, particularly if I knew the spouses—or relatives—well I found it prudent to interview the husband first to acknowledge him as head of the household (a cultural mannerism), but this wasn't always essential.

Gradually I eased into my "new" field of interest. In 1981 I presented a paper at the Rocky Mountain Modern Language Association in Boise, Idaho titled "Rooster Racing in the Río Puerco Valley of New Mexico: 1885–1958." A year later, August 1982, I gave a lecture, "Brujas y brujerías en el Valle del Río Puerco de Nuevo México," at the annual conference of the American Association of Teachers of Spanish and Portuguese (AATSP) in New Orleans. The presentation was under a special session on Oral Hispanic Literature of the United States.

My interests related to my beloved Río Puerco Valley and Guadalupe (aka Ojo del Padre) in particular, the village where I was raised, continued unabated. In 1983 I attended the yearly conference of the American Association of Teachers of Spanish and Portuguese in Boston. There, an unlikely place, I presented a slide show on "Death Comes to Guadalupe: An Hispanic Village on the Río Puerco Valley of New Mexico." The session attracted a large audience—approximately seventy to eighty attendees.

Two years later, July 1985, an exhibit under the theme "Photography Plus" opened to the academic community in the art gallery of Hoag Recital Hall at the University of Southern Colorado. The show featured black and white photographs by Isabel A. Rodríguez a friend and professional photographer from Albuquerque. The portraits highlighted former old-timers of the Río Puerco Valley whom I interviewed and now lived in the Albuquerque environs.

Each photograph included a caption or *dicho*, folk saying that reflected a slice of the interviewees' days in rural New Mexico. One of the citations in an article by Carol Kronwitter, staff writer for the Pueblo-Chieftain newspaper, came from a gentleman who summarized the spirit of life in the hinterland in this way. "As for me, the.life of the rancher during the time we [I] lived on the Río Puerco Valley, as a young man as well as an adult, it's the happiest life that possibly exists." Another saying came from my father; it was one of his favorites. "No hay mal que por bien no venga." (Every cloud has a silver lining.)

The photography exhibit concomitant with comments I received in my campus mail from students, colleagues, and staff attested to an enormous success.

In the meantime the vice president of academic affairs asked me to serve through the summer of 1981 as assistant vice president for research, which I did, but my heart and soul belonged in the classroom. I returned in the fall to the language department and resumed my teaching duties.

By 1984 the university hired a new vice president of academic affairs. Later as he became acquainted with the institution and its faculty, he asked me to serve as interim dean of the College of Liberal and Fine Arts for 1984–1985. Given the confidence he and the president entrusted to me, I accepted to serve even though I had no prior administrative experiences. But by the time I was granted tenure in 1979 I had served on at least twenty university-wide committees that provided me with top to bottom knowledge of the university's infrastructure. Among those committees was the University Commission to Examine the Mission of USC (1976).

After a year as dean, I was asked to serve as Assistant Vice President of Academic and Student Affairs (1985–1986). As I ascended the administrative ladder, I couldn't help but to recall the words of Ramón J. Sender the Spanish novelist who once said to me, "Nasario, one of these days you could become the president of a university . . . which would be a pity." In the intervening time, the former vice president of academic and student affairs who appointed me as dean of the School of Liberal and Fine Arts had assumed the presidency at New Mexico Highlands University. He asked me to join his team, so to speak. Thanks to his invitation I applied and interviewed for the deanship of the School of Liberal and Fine Arts. I was offered the position, signed a contract, and thereby tendered my resignation at the University of Southern Colorado on August 29, 1986.

My thirteen years (1973–1986) at USC, like those at Chatham College in Pittsburgh, were most inspiring and rewarding. My rapport with and appreciation of the students I had the privilege of teaching was uppermost in my mind. Thanks in large measure to them I was honored several times as an Outstanding Faculty Member.

The collegiality among the faculty ranks and administration shall not be overlooked either. Administrators themselves, above all the presidents and vice presidents of academic affairs, never failed to acknowledge faculty's dedication to the students as well as to recognize his or her contributions to scholarship and creative endeavors.

When I departed the University of Southern Colorado, I left behind wonderful students and countless friends both on campus and in the community, some of whom I still stay in touch with thirty-five plus years later. But, after being away from New Mexico for twenty-two years, 1964–1986, (i.e., Spain, Pennsylvania, Illinois, and Colorado), I could now honestly say that I was coming home to my native state. Time, the determiner of all matters, ultimately would tell the tale as to whether leaving Colorado was prudent or not. My maternal grandma's words of wisdom that she invoked from time to time came to mind. "Hijito, quien no ve pa' adelante se queda atrás." (My dear son, he who doesn't look toward the future lags behind.)

The Journey Is Ended

SEVERAL FACULTY MEMBERS AT NEW Mexico Highlands University who were not Las Vegas natives hinted during my interview of an entrenched local culture on campus. "Be forewarned," said a senior professor, "for the Peter Principle might thwart your efforts and initiatives as dean." I had read Laurence Peter's book and was familiar with the concept of individuals who rise in the hierarchy despite their incompetence. I listened courteously to the professor and all voices before and after I assumed the deanship of the School of Liberal and Fine Arts. "Not only that," he continued, "you're likely to be ensnared by the PIN syndrome."

"And what is the pin syndrome?" I asked curiously.

"That's politics, incompetence, and nepotism. Unknown forces will NIP you coming or going," he concluded as he reversed the acronym.

I began my position as deanship on September 1, 1986. I was quick to inform faculty and staff that my maternal great-grandmother was born in Mora, whereas my paternal grandmother came from Pecos. Most faculty members extended me a warm welcome, in particular those in the language department; others were more reticent. Still others rendered their own advice and counsel. I was advised to confer with two or three full professors as a matter of respect since they were long-standing members of the faculty. One in particular was recognized—or lauded—as the university's acknowledged scholar in residence. This drew my attention and I thereby asked my secretary to provide me with his dossier. I carefully perused his publications. His two or three books were vanity press works. Compared to former scholars in Colorado, Pittsburgh, and Illinois where I had taught, I was not duly impressed.

Later on I asked my secretary, a marvelous human being who knew the faculty well, to provide me with the dossier of each faculty member department by department. I vowed to become acquainted with their educational backgrounds, status as teachers, scholars, and their role in community service. Teaching of course was at the forefront. Overall the potpourri of information I gleaned was helpful in assessing the strengths and weaknesses of the faculty.

Step by step I became acquainted with faculty members in their respective departments. These included languages, history, English, art, mass communications, theater, political science, and music. Psychology, sociology, and anthropology completed the litany of disciplines in Liberal and Fine Arts.

Diversity as such had its advantages and disadvantages. More importantly, I was forever conscious not to favor one discipline over another, or to support some faculty while neglecting others. It was a juggling act I learned to play at the University of Southern Colorado. Even so, I had my cast of supporters, naysayers, and detractors. That was nothing new either based on my previous administrative experience.

As dean I advocated that administrators ought to teach a course in one's discipline to show students that we supervisors weren't just pencil pushers and paper shufflers. In my case I taught Beginning Spanish. Being in the classroom gave me an opportunity to evaluate the quality and preparation of incoming freshmen in particular, many of whom hailed from small villages of northern New Mexico and southern Colorado. I enjoyed the dual role and challenge of being a professor and an administrator.

The School of Liberal and Fine Arts was one of several new schools within the university's overall organizational structure of academic programs. There were challenges, of course. Chiefly among them was resistance to change most notably among a few senior faculty members—not an anomaly by any means—who to a great extent tended to be conservative and more inclined to protect their own turf. I was keenly aware of these attitudes and inclinations since I served on the Commission to Examine the Mission of the University of Southern Colorado.

In consulting with faculty of all ranks within the School of Liberal and Fine Arts, there was no unanimous consensus on any given academic program or special event to give the school visibility. Accordingly, in concert with colleagues from several departments, I launched several activities to showcase the school across campus and the community at large. These included a monthly Faculty Lecture Series (1987–1988), a Foreign Film Festival (1988–1989), and later a New Mexico Storytelling Festival. These programs were ancillary to, but supportive of, the school's academic programs.

I headlined the lecture series with "Growing Up in America: A Sense of Belonging." I had shared this topic with southern Colorado audiences under the sponsorship of the American Issues Forum. Faculty who volunteered to be speakers chose their own topics. Of the three programs alluded to above, the lectures drew the largest audiences; they included students, faculty, administrators, and community people.

One individual, not a faculty member, whom I invited to participate in the lecture series, included the legendary Antonia Josefina Apodaca. She was the flamboyant accordion player and talented musician from Rociada, New Mexico, north of Las Vegas where she was born. Even before I arrived at the lecture hall to introduce her, she had the audience dancing in the aisles. She was marvelous. Antonia Apodaca passed away on January 25, 2020.

Attendance at the Foreign Film Festival was mixed. Feedback from attendees ran the gamut from outstanding to fair. The film festival and lecture series were in the evening and primarily ear-marked for interested parties on campus and the local community.

The New Mexico Storytelling Festival, held on Friday and Saturday April 20 and 21, 1990 targeted audiences in the region and nearby northern New Mexico villages. Among them were Mora, Cleveland, Chacón, Peñasco, Wagon Mound, and Springer. Guests were invited free of charge. The multicultural focus of storytellers included Curt Brummett, Larry Littlebird, the late Linda Piper, Pearl Sunrise, and Cleofas Vigil the singer-storyteller from San Cristóbal of northern New Mexico who has also passed away. (A colorful en-tertainer, I met him at a cultural fiesta at the University of Southern Colorado.)

The core of talented individuals from across cultures was phe-nomenal, but the turnout was sparse. The few students who attended were impressed. One student in particular who was present for all the performances said to me, "Dr. García, the storytellers were great! But where was everyone?" I simply shrugged my shoulders.

Storytelling is but one fascinating facet of oral history and folk-lore that I enjoyed in my thirty-plus years of interviewing Hispanic old-timers. Other features include *dichos*, folk sayings, *adivinanzas*, riddles, songs, *alaba(d)os*, religious hymns of praise, *entriegas*, wedding songs, and *chiquiaos*, love quatrains.

My book *Recuerdos de los viejitos: Tales of the Río Puerco* was published in 1987—less than a year after I arrived at Highlands University—by the University of New Mexico Press in collabora-tion with the Historical Society of New Mexico (HSNM). Chief supporters of my oral history undertakings were historians Dr. Myra Ellen Jenkins who wrote the foreword, and Penny Wilson, an active member of HSNM. He was best known for promoting the Cumbres and Toltec Scenic Railroad. Jenkins and Wilson, both of whom have passed away, provided the initial impetus to and unstinted support of my oral history and folklore projects on the Río Puerco Valley where I was raised. Of my thirty-plus books published to date, a dozen of them are based on tape-recorded interviews I conducted in Spanish with Hispanic old-timers from New Mexico, Arizona, California, Colorado, and Texas.

In addition to Jenkins and Wilson the list of historians, allies of my oral history, reads like a who's who in the annals of New Mexico history. The renowned historian Marc Simmons (1937-2023) wrote the foreword to *Brujas, bultos, y brasas: Tales of Witchcraft and the Supernatural in the Pecos Valley* (He also authored the foreword to the award-winning *Hoe, Heaven, and Hell: My Boyhood in Rural New Mexico*.). Tom E. Chávez, best known for his treatises on Spain and United States Independence, penned the preface, a fine piece of writing, to *Fe y tragedias: Faith and Tragedies in Hispanic Villages of New Mexico.*

Other scholars who have endorsed my work, well-known in their respective areas of specialization, are Richard Melzer, Richard Flint, Richard W. Etulain, Robert Tórrez, Estevan Rael-Gálvez, Don Bullis, Ana Pacheco, Anthony J. Cárdenas, Frances Levine, Garland D. Bills, Enrique Lamadrid, and Nancy Owen Lewis, who died in 2022 at the age of seventy-seven. Howard Bryan the journalist turned historian, Estevan Arellano, and Tom J. Steele, all of whom have also left this earth, endorsed my work as well.

The eminent folklorist Rubén Cobos, an avid fan of my fieldwork on folklore, wrote the foreword to *Más Antes: Hispanic Folklore of the Río Puerco Valley*. "Más antes," he inscribed, "is a marvelous mosaic of traditions, language, and oral history and literature that represents the rich legacy the residents of the Río Puerco Valley have left for all to enjoy."

Two folklorists and/or oral historians in their own right who have championed my work are master teacher Larry Torres from

Taos, and Esther Córdova May whose books on her native Cuba, New Mexico left a mark of their own. She passed away in 2023.

Creative writers such as the late Sabine R. Ulibarrí who composed the preface to *Abuelitos–Tales of the Río Puerco Valley* lauded my bringing the viejitos' stories to the fore. Here is an excerpt of his kindhearted words:

> It is necessary to know where you come from to know
> where you are and what you are, in order to know where
> you are headed and who you will be. Nasario García
> knows very well where he comes from. That is why his
> road in life is well marked. Kindness and loyalty have
> taken Nasario to the land that saw him born and that taught
> him to want to bring to light the history of a corner of New
> Mexico and the people who made that history. A history
> lost in the past until now.

Jim Sagel, a transplant from Colorado and raconteur who settled in Española, was a close friend and wonderful human being. He authored the preface to *Tata: A Voice from the Río Puerco*. "To read these pages [*Tata*]," he wrote, "is to listen along with the younger Nasario, as his elder namesake recreates a universe full of pride, spirituality, tragedy, and fun. He leaves nothing out of the stories, which touch on everything from *brujerías* (witchcraft) to *borracheras* (drunken sprees). With a simple eloquence, he relates how life on the ranch was difficult and often dangerous, but never lonely." My father's stories date back to his childhood in the Río Puerco Valley where he was born in 1912, and where I, Nasario García, spent my childhood.

Demetria Martínez's poetics in the preface to *Comadres: Hispanic Women of the Río Puerco Valley* ring as true today as they did back in 1997. As she says, "The Women recall their lives in imagery uncorrupted by the often clinical and abstract psychobabble that dominates so much of today's discourse." And there is the inimitable John Nichols (1940-2023) who penned the foreword to *¡Chistes! Hispanic Humor of Northern New Mexico and Southern Colorado*. For him "laughter never stops. The Spanish versions of these tales are particularly funny, pungent, and interesting because they are recounted in colorful local vernacular that are heard nowhere else on earth."

But not to be lost in the mix are Rudolfo Anaya's generous words to *Brujas, bultos, y brasas–Tales of Witchcraft and the Supernatural in the Pecos Valley*. "As a child I heard many of these stories, *cuentos* about witches the people told to entertain us. Some were scary enough to make us behave. This book not only entertains, it helps preserve a very important element of Nuevo Mexicano culture."

The eloquent words of praise by poets Anne Valley-Fox and V. B. "Barrett" Price pertaining to *Lágrimas: Poems of Joy and Sorrow*, together with the late E. A. "Tony" Mares who wrote the preface to *Tiempos lejanos: Poetic Images from the Past*, still bring joy to my heart.

Two popular New Mexican novelists who have lauded my creative accomplishments are Catalina Claussen and Sue Boggio. The latter's words of praise regarding *No More Bingo, Comadre! Stories* are heartwarming. "A uniquely New Mexican collection of stories with indelible characters exploring cultural collisions with humor tinged with pathos." Claussen's words extolling my poetry are just as pleasing. "*Lagrimas*," she wrote, "is told in a series of poems written in Spanish and English, breathing life into a village [Nasario's] that was abandoned more than half a century ago. A delight to read."

Overall inspiration of my work among historians, folklorists, and creative writers transcends New Mexico. Along with Eduardo Garrigues, Spanish novelist and former ambassador to Namibia, there are Rolando Hinojosa-Smith, novelist and short story writer, and Nicolás "Nic" Kanellos, both from Texas. Francisco Jiménez, short story writer, and Francisco Lomelí, specialist in Chicano literature, both of whom reside in California, have been quite complimentary of my work. Gary D. Keller, general editor, *Bilingual Review*, and Chuck Tatum, literary critic, residents from Arizona, have championed my efforts. Last, but by no means least, there is Erlinda Gonzales-Berry, Chicano literary critic and New Mexico native who now lives in Oregon. She rounds out the forgoing authors and scholars whose support of my oral history or creative writing endeavors throughout the years is hereby acknowledged.

I would be remiss if I did not acknowledge the loyal support of my readers, many of whom I know personally but others, the majority of them, I have never met. And of course there are the omnipresent reviewers whose kind words and critiques have emboldened me to pursue my interest in oral history as well as to be a better storyteller and poet.

The eight or nine publishers whether instate or outside our borders, namely, New Mexico, Texas, New York, and Pennsylvania, cannot be overlooked. Without them and their staff no book could have seen the light of day for either me or my readers to enjoy.

While dean at Highlands University, as mentioned earlier, I endeavored to give visibility to the School of Liberal and Fine Arts by virtue of organizing a variety of cultural events on campus. But I also participated in professional activities away from the university. I continued to underline the importance of scholarship concomitant with good teaching.

I tried my best, too, in concert with the faculty, to improve academic programs and the working environment for them and the staff to take pleasure in. Replacing decrepit wooden office desks, purchasing state of art equipment, upgrading curricular offerings, at the same time keeping students' needs and interests uppermost in mind, was a top priority.

In 1991, my fifth year as dean of the School of Liberal and Fine Arts, I was elected national president of the prominent American Association of Teachers of Spanish and Portuguese (AATSP) founded in 1917. In its long-standing history I was only the second New Mexican to enjoy that prestigious honor (Sabine R. Ulibarrí is the other native son). The communications and public relations officer on campus issued a press release with regards to my election. This was after all a propitious feather in Highlands University's hat. Immediately I received letters of congratulations from friends and colleagues from across the country. I even heard from United States Senator Jeff Bingaman on January 23, 1990, congratulating me on the presidency.

Yet, except for a few faculty members on campus who congratulated me viva voce, the "house" was silent. This tacit and inexplicable silence was unprecedented in my academic career. I was profoundly saddened given how hard I worked to discharge my duties as dean and as an academic. I truly believed, however naively, that as an administrator you led by example. That is why I stayed active in professional organizations, published books and scholarly articles in addition to being a conscientious part-time teacher.

I reflected on my past five years in administration during which time I worked with a number of respectable individuals. Just the same I wondered whether all my efforts in leading the most visible contingency of faculty and staff on campus had been to no avail. The words of the senior professor—a non-native—who forewarned me upon my arrival on campus that I'd be "ensnared" by the so-called PIN (Politics, Incompetence, and Nepotism) syndrome rang loud and clear. But I refused to stand in judgment. I left that notion at other people's doorsteps to ponder. My father's words of wisdom, "No hay que juzgar el hatajo por lo que hacen uno o dos chivos" (You must not judge the entire flock by the actions of one or two goats [scoundrels]) came to mind.

The fall semester of 1991–1992 had arrived. I gladly returned to my tenured position in the language department. The classroom, after all, is where my heart and soul belonged. Besides, my health had taken a toll. It was time to resume my teaching, regain a sense of purpose, and to continue my fieldwork in oral history and folklore with the viejitos. That same academic year I published my second book on oral history, *Abuelitos: Stories of the Río Puerco Valley*. In 1994 *Tata: A Voice from the Río Puerco* saw the light. *Tata*, as alluded to earlier, is a collection of oral stories that my father (*tata*) shared with me apropos of his life in the Río Puerco Valley where he was born. Five (5) additional books on the topic of oral history, plus *Pláticas: Conversations with Hispano Writers of New Mexico*, ed. *Cantares: Canticles and Poems of Youth*, Fray Angélico Chávez, and a textbook by Prentice Hall (eight total), were published during my ten years (1991–2001) as a professor at Highlands University. Most of my scholarship was undertaken and brought to fruition on weekends and during the summer months since my primary focus throughout the academic year, was—and continued to be—the students.

The most heart-breaking aspect is that many of the scholastic problems freshmen faced were reminiscent of those that plagued me when I started at the University of New Mexico. A case in point was the interference of Spanish in the pronunciation of words versus English that I detailed previously in this narrative. This added to their predicament even though their knowledge of Spanish, their parents' native language, in many cases was rudimentary, at best.

Many students, the first in their family to attend college, came from households with modest economic means whose deep cultural roots rested in northern New Mexico. A number of them were in my classes to fulfill a curriculum requirement. Others were there to "recuperate" or learn the language of their parents who had insisted, rightly or wrongly, that their son or daughter should learn English if they wanted to succeed in society. The parents did not foresee the benefits of being bilingual let alone multilingual. Their sons and daughters thought differently, and those of us who taught languages reinforced the value of knowing more than one language.

Teaching twelve hours or four different courses even for full professors who were tenured, was not unusual at Highlands University. I taught an occasional graduate course or seminar with fewer students who were enrolled in the Southwest Studies Program. But, said courses demanded much more time in terms of class preparation, examinations, and grading research papers than did beginning or intermediate courses. Heavy teaching loads at New Mexico's regional institutions by no means were atypical. Emphasis was predominantly on teaching.

All the same—and paradoxically—for faculty to be considered for advancement in rank, pay increases or tenure, scholarship and community service comprised an integral part of the overall evaluation criteria. Most faculty found the latter ironic since administrators by and large had little to boast about in terms of scholarship and/ or community service. A respected professor on campus once said to me facetiously, "The only claim to fame by most academic affairs administrators is their name, home address, and social security number."

All things considered, I served on state and national boards. For years I was a member of the New Mexico Endowment for the Humanities and a lecturer on their Speakers Bureau and Chautauqua Programs. Away from our state, I was a consultant to the College Board and Educational Testing Services, Princeton, New Jersey, and North Central Association of Colleges and Schools. Lastly, I was a board member of the Southwest Oral History Association that praised my thirty-plus years of rescuing from oblivion stories of Hispanic old-timers of New Mexico and elsewhere in the American Southwest.

A preponderance of my fieldwork was brought to fruition thanks to major and mini research grants. My first major grant was the Southern Fellowship Research Grant (1980–1981) under the auspices of Emory University mentioned in chapter 11. For one of my later projects thanks to a generous grant from the Center for Regional Studies at the University of New Mexico I conducted a series of interviews (in Spanish) with Hispanic old-timers of the Río Pecos Valley. All of the informants came from the villages of Villanueva, Sena, El Pueblo, San José, Ribera, etc. Once transcribed and translated into English the interviews led to the publication in 1999 of *Brujas, bultos, y brasas: Tales of Witchcraft and the Supernatural in the Pecos Valley*.

In 2000 I published *Pláticas: Conversations with Hispano Writers of New Mexico*, mentioned earlier in this chapter, an unprecedented work that highlighted the likes of Sabine R. Ulibarrí and Rudolfo Anaya. As stated in the foreword by Francisco A. Lomelí, a well-known student of Chicano literature, "The authors interviewed for this work clearly embody important links to a Hispanic past and are some of the best writers in contemporary New Mexico."

With regard to my fieldwork related to the viejitos, I shared it with my students in courses such as "A Survey of Hispanic Culture of New Mexico." In doing so, above all if a student came from one of the villages in the Río Pecos Valley, he or she was able to recognize one or two interviewees including a relative here and there. In the process, the students learned a facet or two about family customs or rituals once popular in their family but no longer celebrated due to lack of interest in or negligence of cultural traditions in northern New Mexico.

Apart from sharing folkloric stories in the classroom that I collected from old-timers, I launched in 1998–1999 a lecture series on campus headlined "Let's Revive Hispanic Culture." The topics I discussed (I was the lone lecturer) ran the gamut from fiestas (i.e., drinking, frolicking, and dancing), old-fashioned courtships and weddings, witchcraft and the supernatural, to rooster racing. Guests in the audience were invited to share their own family stories or histories. One student in particular said to me after one of my lectures, "Dr. García, I've heard my grandparents talk about some of the same cultural events when they were young."

The *Journal North*, under the auspices of the *Albuquerque Journal*, published a number of articles that featured my lectures at Highlands University. Such publications reached readers throughout northern New Mexico who otherwise may not have had the opportunity to attend the lectures on campus.

At the risk of proselytizing, I endeavored to inculcate a sense of pride in students with regard to their ancestral roots, but at the same time strove to motivate them to succeed in their studies. I told them the story of a Hispanic professor, a rabble-rouser from New Mexico who was teaching in Colorado. Because I had a doctorate from the University of Pittsburgh, he had the unmitigated audacity to accuse me of having been born with a silver spoon in my mouth. "Quite the contrary," I retorted, "I was born with a tortilla in my mouth." The students chuckled. They got the point. "You have to work for what you get, right?" a student blurted on impulse as if to come to my defense.

Whenever appropriate, I shared personal stories connected to my upbringing in rural New Mexico, which included starting school in a one-room adobe school house with one teacher and eight grades—first through eighth. They were impressed. As a result, several students suggested that I write and recount my own stories whether in prose or in poetry; they thought that my experiences were just as important and motivating as those I had collected from old-timers.

I heeded their advice. I wrote and published *Tiempos lejanos: Poetic Images from the Past*, my first book of poetry, and later authored

The Naked Rainbow and Other Stories: El arco iris desnudo y otros cuentos. Both bilingual works stem from my students' encouragement to write about my own experiences. They depict facets of my childhood in rural New Mexico that reflect in part my students' own cultural and proud milieu of northern New Mexico.

Toward the end of my teaching career, I asked students in one of my classes to share what they were doing to preserve and advance their culture. A student without hesitation raised his hand and said, "Oh, I go to Taco-Bell once a week and buy myself a burrito grande." His classmates laughed, but alas he was serious. For a fleeting moment I thought to myself, "If his words are from the heart, they are better than a calculated statement of hypocrisy."

I am pleased to say that my teaching days at Highlands University from 1991 to 2001 started on a positive note and ended likewise. In March 1992 at the end of my first year in the classroom I was initiated—thanks to some of my students—into the New Mexico Highlands University Chapter of Phi Eta Sigma Freshman Honor Society in recognition of excellence in teaching.

Ten years later, in 2001, at the cusp of retirement, Glen W. Davidson, the provost, organized a dinner to honor several individuals in the academic community. He thanked me publicly for my service to the university: my teaching, community service, and in particular my scholarly work. He was a scholar in his own right who appreciated the numerous books I had published during my ten-year tenure as a professor. Above all else, Dr. Davidson was a veritable gentleman.

From my early teaching days at Chatham College in Pittsburgh, and all through my academic career, students were my first and foremost priority. They were always the glowing light and inspiration. Because of them even when I found myself in the doldrums, I went to class well-prepared. I never short-changed them. I forever felt strongly that faculty members truly made a difference in the success of students' personal and professional lives. Professors whether excellent teachers or not were looked upon as the paragons of knowledge.

When I retired after thirty-six years in academia, I did so without any regrets. I was strict with and demanding of my students, but I constantly strove to be fair. I felt quite content then, as I do now, that my performance in the classroom at all times was above reproach. As a teacher I was the beneficiary of numerous teaching awards. I trust it's principally because my students recognized and appreciated my dedication to them and the subjects I taught. As my career ended, I left an erstwhile profession with a clear conscience. I walked out of the classroom for the last time a happy teacher.

Then and Now

AS I GLANCE AT THE educational map that I traversed starting in the Río Puerco Valley, I do so with a profound sense of pride and satisfaction. Though it seems like eons ago, nothing looms more vividly among the mesas and volcanic plugs on the desert-like horizon than the one-room adobe schoolhouse—grades one through eight—where I started school in Rincón del Cochino.

The night before I embarked on my long and unforeseen educational journey, excitement filled the air in Mom's kitchen. The image of Big Chief on my Big Chief Tablet appeared to sport a smile. Even the box of Crayolas and pencil, my other precious school supplies on top of the dining table, sparkled with joy. Dad's offer to sharpen the pencil with his pocket knife added to the enthusiasm.

I can still picture myself the next day riding my uncle Antonio's eight-passenger school bus bouncing up and down on winding dirt roads dodging prairie dogs as we headed for La Mesa School. The year was 1943. That scene at this very moment evokes a dramatic contrast to the elevator I rode the winter of 1966 to attend my first class on the sixteenth floor of the forty-two-story Cathedral of Learning at the University of Pittsburgh. My voyage in the classroom that began at La Mesa School ended on December 20, 1972. On that fateful day far away from my one-room adobe school—house I was awarded my PhD.

Upon reflection my life as a student is filled with both joy and despair, but I never succumbed to adversity irrespective of its nature, magnitude or seeming insignificance. Destiny in and of itself is unpredictable, but hope at all times comprised part of my innermost motivation. Whenever I felt dejected, my father's words of wisdom and optimism were uplifting. "Mientras que uno está vivo, hay esperanza." (As long as one is alive, there's hope.)

Although my parents' ancestral roots in New Mexico transcend several centuries, they both came from poor farming-ranching families with virtually no opportunity to pursue an education. Mom and Dad spoke Spanish, their native language, but they could neither read nor write it. Worse yet, they felt estranged in an English-speaking world since English was—and is indeed—a foreign language in New Mexico. To see them purchase groceries by glancing at food images on canned goods was heartbreaking. Episodes of this nature had a profound effect on me as a young boy in the countryside and later in Albuquerque.

When we moved to Albuquerque's Martíneztown from the Río Puerco Valley, I started third grade at Santa Barbara School. My English competency was virtually nonexistent. To make matters worse, my teacher was mean-spirited, not to mention the fact that Hispanics at school ridiculed what little English I spoke. I became self-conscious, discouraged, and wanted to quit school. Mom was sympathetic, whereas my father predictably was more philosophical. "No hay mal que por bien no venga," (Every cloud has a silver lining) he uttered at the dinner table.

Miss Padilla a caring fourth-grade teacher who was bilingual eased somewhat my discomfort and psychological stress in the classroom. In retrospect she was special in the entire cadre of my teachers in the Albuquerque School System.

To this day I can recite with rare exception nearly all of my teachers' names both for good and unflattering reasons. At the same time, it saddens me to say that most teachers were strapped with too many classes and students to teach. I felt then as I do today that they were (and are) overworked and underpaid.

To exacerbate matters, at times the teaching atmosphere was

challenging and not conducive to learning. The presence of rival gangs was intimidating if not outright disruptive for both the teachers and students. Other mitigating factors, to wit, lack of motivation among students, added to the overall malaise. I could not help but to sympathize with all teachers whether they were good, fair, or indifferent.

I myself was not a good student. Somehow I survived (barely) the academic and social throes of junior high and high school. It was not until my senior year (1954–1955) at Valley High School, a new school, that I felt as though I belonged to and was an integral part of the student body. Having new administrators and staff, coupled with caring and enthusiastic teachers added to the overall positive atmosphere.

I was among the first graduating class (about 115 students) of 1955. My proud parents were in the audience (I am the eldest of eight siblings and the first and only one ever to finish high school.). Those fleeting but joyful moments helped motivate me in furthering my education. Seventeen years later, 1972, sadly and by sheer coincidence my mother passed away on the same day, May 25, a scant few months before I was awarded the PhD. My days as a student at the University of Pittsburgh ended on a quiet note.

All through my long-standing teaching career, the classroom became the stage and students my supporting cast. I the professor-actor played multiple roles in teaching the rudiments and intricacies of Spanish literature: prose, poetry, and drama. In addition, I taught folklore, oral history, and the Spanish language of northern New Mexico. I endeavored to teach each of the foregoing genres with equal aplomb and passion.

I learned that the sharing of one's knowledge should not be subservient to other aspects of the academic world. Equally as important was to challenge students to bare their intellectual souls to benefit them as well as their classmates.

Academia is not a perfect world. Just like any other profession, it comprises human beings who are susceptible to human frailty. Yet for me the academic world was intellectually challenging, unpredictable, devoid of tedium, and ideally suited for my temperament.

The day I retired I left behind a noble profession that I thoroughly enjoyed. That momentous spring morning in 2001, surrounded by my last class of students, I bid goodbye to each one and to thirty-six years of teaching with peace of mind and nary a day of regrets or apologies. As the last student left the classroom, I glanced at the empty desks. The scene somehow propelled me back in time and space to my one-room adobe school in the Río Puerco Valley. Suddenly Plato's words from my sophomore world literature class at the University of New Mexico came to me. "If a man neglects education, he walks lame to the end of his life."

Students were the lifeline to my pedagogical happiness. Whatever modest success I experienced in and outside the classroom I am primarily indebted to them. They kept me young, alert, and even current on their latest lingo, jokes, hair styles, and dress habits. As a professor, I had the best of two worlds—theirs and mine.

Beyond My Adobe Schoolhouse

APPENDIX A

Foreign Countries Visited

Here in alpha order are the foreign countries that I visited during my academic career. Of particular note are the one-month visits that my wife and I made to Spain and Portugal over a period of fifteen straight summers (1986–2001).

Africa	Holland
Argentina	Hungary
Belgium	Italy
Canada	Mexico
China	Norway
Costa Rica	Peru
Czech Republic	Portugal
Denmark	Puerto Rico
England	Slovenia
France	Spain
Germany	Sweden
Guatemala	Switzerland

APPENDIX B

Memorable Career Moments

In life many of us claim to have a favorite or lucky number. For me that number is thirty-six. First of all, I was born in 1936. Thirty-six years later, 1972, I received my PhD. Lastly, I devoted thirty-six years (1965–2001) to academia before I retired.

My university career, both as a student and professor, is filled with myriad moments that are close to my heart. I hereby wish to share in ascending order a brief synopsis of some of those special occurrences as well as to recognize certain individuals who made a difference throughout my educational experience.

Dr. Albert R. Lopes, Professor of Languages, University of New Mexico, 1957–1963

Dr. Albert R. Lopes was a superb teacher who touched the lives of scores of students during his long-standing career at the University of New Mexico. (Perhaps his most famous student was President Jimmy E. Carter whom Dr. Lopes taught at the United States Naval Academy during World War II while he served in the US Navy.). He taught Spanish, Italian, German, and French (he also knew Latin), but, more importantly, he introduced, taught, and developed a thriving Portuguese program. He started with beginning courses that blossomed into a minor, a major, and ultimately a master's degree in Portuguese and Luso-Brazilian literatures. When Dr. Lopes retired (circa 1967) the Portuguese program enjoyed a national reputation.

In recognition of his tireless devotion to Portuguese, the government of Portugal in 1967 named Dr. Albert R. Lopes Knight Commander of the Order of Prince Henry the Navigator. I am proud and fortunate to have been one of Dr. Lopes's students and protégés. He was an inspiration to me.

Ramón J. Sender, Professor of Spanish, University of New Mexico, 1959–1961

I can still picture the distinguished Spanish writer as he walked up and down the hallways before class started. With suit jacket draped over his shoulders and hands folded behind his back he greeted you with a cordial albeit stern look on his face. That was his disposition; he hardly ever smiled. I studied two courses with Professor Sender: the Spanish Novel, and Contemporary Spanish Literature. He was a serious professor in the classroom, but little by little I discovered— as I'm sure I could vouch for some of my classmates—that he had a wry sense of humor.

At the beginning of a semester Professor Sender started calling roll. "Señorita Chávez," and you had to respond, "Su servidor." He continued. "Señor Torpe, señor Torpe," he repeated, but there was no response. At that very instant I heard someone whisper to Thorpe. "I think he's calling your name," and he stood up. "Señor Profesor, soy yo, pero el nombre es Thorpe, Thorpe" (Sir, that's me, but the name is Thorpe, Thorpe), he repeated as if to make his point. "¡Vaya! A usted lo único que lo salvó fue la hache" (Come now! The only thing that saved you is the letter *h*), don Ramón exclaimed sarcastically. He was quick witted. Some students giggled under their breath. They undoubtedly knew that in New Mexico *torpe* means stupid or dimwitted.

Yet the most memorable moment for me occurred when I went to pick up a letter of recommendation that Professor Sender had written in my behalf. As he handed me the letter he said with a smile, "Nasario, algún día podrías llegar a ser rector de una universidad" (Nasario, one day you could become the president of a university), and he paused, "lo cual sería una lástima" (which would be a pity). By then we had gotten to know each other. We got along well. I felt fortunate since he was a complex personality, but deep inside he was a compassionate human being. I have fond memories of Ramón J. Sender.

Doctoral Courses, University of Granada, Spain, 1964–1965

My year of doctoral courses (*cursos monográficos*) at the University of Granada in the School of Humanities (*Filosofía y Letras*) looms as one of the most enlightening and gratifying periods of my graduate studies. The professors were excellent given the fact that one or two of them had to moonlight to augment their meager salaries (e.g., my advisor though he was a full professor and held the *cátedra*, tenure worked as a baker).

The most rewarding part of the academic year was the linguistic courses I studied under the eminent linguist Dr. Manuel Alvar López. Because of his keen interest in colonial Spanish of northern New Mexico, we became friends (he was touched that I was also a López on my mother's side), a rarity at that time among Spanish professors and students. For two or three years after my departure from Granada, we exchanged Christmas greetings. The summer of 1991, I phoned him while I was in Madrid, but he had a lecture in Logroño so we couldn't get together. I then sent him a copy of my first book on oral history *Recuerdos de los viejitos: Tales of the Río Puerco*. Since my days in Granada I never saw him again. Dr. Alvar died in 2001 at age seventy-eight (See Postscript, chapter 7).

Robert S. McNamara, Secretary of Defense, Chatham College, 1966

My indoctrination into academia at Chatham College in 1965 was exciting, but little did I realize that certain events at this wonderful institution would add to the overall euphoria. One such moment occurred at graduation in the spring of 1966. The honorable Robert S. McNamara, Secretary of Defense under presidents John F. Kennedy and Lyndon Johnson, was the commencement speaker. He also presented his daughter with her diploma. To have a guest of high stature such as Secretary McNamara was exceptional. The campus was abuzz with excitement.

Jorge Luis Borges, Carnegie Institute of Technology, circa 1967

Carnegie Institute of Technology (CIT) was at the point of becoming Carnegie Mellon University. I attended a lecture co-sponsored by the University of Pittsburgh and CIT. The speaker was the renowned Argentinian writer Jorge Luis Borges who at that time was a visiting lecturer at Harvard University. Right before Borges was to speak, a young man escorted him to the front row near the lectern. Borges was already losing his eyesight. He spoke on the status of contemporary authors in Spanish America but did not include his own writings. At the end of his presentation, a student addressed Borges. "Professor Borges, I have read your short stories and poetry, and it appears that you may have been influenced by so-and-so's writings (I don't recall the writer's name). Would you like to comment?" Borges of course knew English. That being the case, he responded, "I can tell by the voice that you're a young man and are seated to my left a few rows away. As to your question and the writer you mentioned, it's a good thought, but I've never read his works." A chuckle reverberated throughout the hall. Borges was respectful, but he also showed he had a sense of humor.

Ruby Dee and Ossie Davis, Chatham College, circa 1968

A noteworthy program at Chatham College was the Artists in Residence. Actors Ruby Dee and Ossie Davis the talented husband and wife team conducted workshops for students in theater and the performing arts. In the evenings Ms. Dee and her husband offered performances on campus sponsored by the administration for students and the academic community to attend free of charge. Such activities by artists, including scholars and lecturers, were common and popular year-round on campus.

Awarded PhD, the University of Pittsburgh, 1972

In 1966 (winter trimester) I enrolled in my first class at the University of Pittsburgh. To take a course on occasion concomitant with teaching fulltime at Chatham College was an intellectual challenge. Most professors in the Department of Hispanic Languages and Literatures at my future alma mater were regular faculty members; others were visiting scholars from Spain, England, Scotland, and Latin America. Together they provided a wide spectrum of expertise in Spanish and Spanish American literatures. One of highpoints was graduate seminars taught in the beautifully decorated Nationality Rooms (e.g., Italian, French). This was impressive and unprecedented in my educational career but being awarded my PhD at the University of Pittsburgh turned out to be a bittersweet experience. I had planned to fly my parents to celebrate the joyous moment. Regrettably, my mother passed away in May 1972 so in deference to her and her memory I did not attend commencement exercises that were held in December 1972.

Teaching Excellence Awards, University of Southern Colorado, 1973–1986

For the academic years 1975–1976 and 1976–1977, I was nominated by the Students National Education Association as Educator (SNEA) of the Year for "teaching excellence and guidance in the classroom." I was profoundly honored to be recognized by the SNEA.

Thereafter on three different academic years, 1977–1978, 1981–1982, and 1982–1983, during my tenure at the University of Southern Colorado in Pueblo, I was recognized for my teaching excellence and outstanding service to the university. The nominations came either from students, my department chairperson, or the administration. The president and academic vice president yearly hosted a formal dinner/banquet and presented faculty members with a bronze plaque called an Owl Award. The vice president never failed to write a letter to the honorees prior to the dinner. For example, on April 28,

1982, I received a letter that characterized the spirit of the award. "I congratulate you warmly on being selected as an Outstanding Faculty member of 1981–1982. The President and the Deans and I look forward to congratulating you personally on May 10."

White House Conference on Libraries and Information Services (WHCLIS), Washington, DC, 1979

In 1979, six years after I joined the faculty at the University of Southern Colorado, Ms. Anne Marie Falsone, Deputy State Librarian Colorado State Library, invited me to serve on the Colorado Commission on Libraries. That same year I was selected to represent Colorado as a delegate-at-large at the WHCLIS. In October a letter came to me from United States Senator Claiborne Pell, Rhode Island, and US Representative William D. Ford, Michigan, "As a delegate to the White House Conference," they wrote, "we would like to invite you to testify before the joint hearing. We would particularly like you to focus on library and information services in fulfillment of continuing education." Their invitation came as total surprise, so, in consultation with library personnel at the state and local levels, I decided to testify on "Illiteracy Among Our Elders in the United States." On November 20, the day after I appeared before the committee, excerpts of my presentation were published on the front page of the *Washington Star*, the forerunner to the *Washington Post*. I was pleased to have testified on a subject of genuine concern to me. Other members of the Pell and Ford committee were the honorable Senators Ted Kennedy, Massachusetts, Jacob Javits, New York, and John Brademas from Indiana.

Former Colorado State Penitentiary Inmate Earns a Medical Degree, 1982

To have taught at the Colorado State Penitentiary (the old CSP facility) in Cañon City to this day remains indelible in my bank of classroom memories. My experience mirrors those teaching days at the Federal/State Prison in Illinois when I was a professor at Northern Illinois University—with one notable and rewarding exception. One of my students at the CSP serving a long-term sentence for murdering his parents in due time earned an associate in arts degree. With strong letters of recommendation from professors like me who taught at the prison, in due course was paroled. He subsequently attended the University of Southern Colorado. There he excelled in his program of studies with emphasis on premed and Spanish. After he received his bachelor of science degree, and again with support from faculty members, he applied for and was accepted into the medical school at the University of Colorado at Denver. He earned a doctorate of medicine in 1982. His accomplishments were impressive to say the least given the oppressive environment inmates endure in penal institutions. I was very proud that he was one of my students both at the prison as well as at the University of Southern Colorado. His accomplishments defied reality and redefined hope for many inmates.

Colorado Congress of Foreign Language Teachers Scholarship Award, 1983

For a number of years I was an active member of the Colorado Congress of Foreign Language Teachers (CCFT). I served on the board, presented research papers at conferences, and authored several articles including one titled "La cultura hispánica en los Estados Unidos—enraizada, no muerta." (Hispanic culture in the United States, deeply rooted, not dead) published in *PEALS*, a newsletter of the organization.

On March 4–5, 1983, I was presented the distinguished Scholarship Award at the CCFLT's annual conference held at the Broadmoor Hotel in Colorado Springs. Such an honor went to an individual who had contributed to the foreign language profession through published works or curricular development. Dan Martínez, at that time a retired District 60 language and social studies specialist in Pueblo, Colorado, who made the presentation, praised my work. "Nasario has assisted the Pueblo public schools in evaluating curricular materials from a cultural, linguistic and historical point of view. . . . His publications of books and papers are too numerous to mention except that special note must be made of the reader *Nuevos Horizontes*, published in 1982 by D. C. Heath and Company and co-edited by Nasario and Dr. José B. Fernández."

President of the American Association of Teachers of Spanish and Portuguese (AATSP), 1991

In 1965, while teaching at Chatham College in Pittsburgh, I joined the AATSP. Twenty-five years later with support from friends and colleagues across the continental United States and Hawaii, I was elected vice president and served as president in 1991. I was only the second native New Mexican to serve in that capacity (Sabine R. Ulibarrí is the other native son) since the association was founded in 1917. Being a New Mexican, I was honored to serve in that capacity of the prestigious language organization. As president I was invited to speak at several AATSP chapters and/or universities in California, Texas, Minnesota, Missouri, and Wyoming. Whether at a university or public schools, I emphasized the importance of teaching Spanish and Portuguese and the multilingual benefits therein for students whatever career they pursued.

In July 1991 I was among a group of scholars, both Spaniards and Americans, invited to Toledo, Spain, to celebrate the Inauguración del Programa de Verano (Quincentennial Summer Program) para Maestros Norteamericanos de Español. The program, which attracted more than 200 teachers, was organized by the Sociedad Estatal del V Centenario and the Fundación Ortega y Gasset in Madrid. I was proud to share information with the teachers regarding the long-standing history of the Spanish language and culture that we have enjoyed in northern New Mexico since the sixteenth century. As president of the AATSP I was greatly pleased to represent New Mexico.

Phi Eta Sigma Honorary Society, New Mexico Highlands University, 1992

On February 14, 1992, Troy Satterfield, president of New Mexico Highlands University Chapter of Phi Eta Sigma Honorary Society, and Charles J. Searcy, faculty advisor, wrote me a letter. It read in part, "It is our great pleasure to inform you that the members of Phi Eta Sigma Freshman Honor Society have elected you as an honorary member in recognition of your excellence in teaching and your demonstrated interest in the education of students. . . . Students who have had the good fortune to have been enrolled in one or more of your classes have benefited from your good teaching in the classroom and from your willingness to give your time and effort whenever needed to assist and encourage them in their professional development. On their behalf, we are pleased to have this opportunity to say, 'Thank you.'" Needless to say, I was delighted at the news. My wife and I attended an induction dinner on March 8, 1992. What a marvelous way to begin anew my teaching career after serving seven years in administration, the last five at Highlands University.

"Hispanic Presence in the United States," Universidad Complutense de Madrid, 1993

On May 5, 1993, Eduardo Garrigues the Spanish consul in Los Angeles invited me and other scholars to participate in the Curso de Verano (Summer Program) sponsored by the Universidad Complutense de Madrid. The *curso* was directed by Eduardo Garrigues himself at San Lorenzo de El Escorial outside Madrid from July 19–23. Other participants came from California, Arizona, and Spain. They addressed a variety of topics related to the "Presencia hispánica en el Sudoeste de los Estados Unidos: Una nueva frontera" (Hispanic Presence in the [American] Southwest: A New Frontier). I spoke on the "Conservación de la lengua y las tradiciones españolas en Nuevo México" (The Conservation of the Spanish language and Traditions of New Mexico). The curso was the perfect venue to talk about the strong cultural and linguistic ties between Spain and northern New Mexico whose richness dates back to the sixteenth century.

New Mexicans Meet with Prince Felipe in Madrid, 1998

In February 1998 Eduardo Garrigues, the Spanish consul in Los Angeles and board member of El Rancho de las Golondrinas in Santa Fe, arranged for a contingency of board members and staff to assemble at Casa América in Madrid. A few of us delivered lectures on the history, culture, and language vis-à-vis Spain's presence in northern New Mexico. But the highpoint was a private meeting with His Royal Highness, Don Felipe VI de Borbón, Príncipe de Asturias, who is now the King of Spain. On that momentous occasion George Paloheimo, former director of El Rancho de las Golondrinas, presented the prince with a copy of *The Exposition on the Province of New Mexico, 1812*, by Don Pedro Baptista Pino translated and edited by Adrian Bustamante and Marc Simmons. His Royal Highness authored a prefatory letter to the edition. An imposing figure at six feet, six inches tall, he was affable, outgoing, and a genuine caballero. It was a delight to meet him.

Zía Award, University of New Mexico, 1999

"The Zía Award honors New Mexico residents with a University of New Mexico degree who have distinguished themselves in any one or more of the following categories: philanthropic endeavors, public office, service to the University, community and volunteer activities, and–or business professional fields, or educational fields." I was pleased to have been selected as one of the honorees for 1999. Present at the banquet was Marie Hayes, a popular teacher at Valley High School the first year (1954–1955) of its founding. I was among the school's first graduating class of 1955.

The Duke and Duchess of Alburquerque (Spain) in Old Town (la Plaza Vieja), 2006

In 2006 the Duke and Duchess of Alburquerque, Ionnes Osoio y Beltrán de Lis, and Blanca Suelves Figueroa, came from Spain to Albuquerque to help celebrate the Duke City's 300th anniversary. They were joined by the Marquis and Marquise of Charity, Gonzalo Ulloa Suelves, and the Marquesa Mercedes Llanza Figueroa. At Martin Chávez's behest, the city mayor at that time, I was asked to give our distinguished guests a tour of historic Old Town Plaza, la Plaza Vieja. I escorted the Duke and Marquis (someone else accompanied the Duchess and Marquise). We visited the San Felipe de Neri Church, the oldest church (1793) in Albuquerque, the Casa de Armijo, currently La Placita Restaurant, built in 1706, for several generations occupied by the Armijo family. El Duque de Alburquerque and El Marqués de la Caridad were very attentive and interested in the historical relationship between New Mexico and Spain. They thoroughly enjoyed the one-hour tour. Both were the consummate gentleman. Before they departed to join their wives, I presented each one with a signed copy of *Albuquerque: ¡Feliz Cumpleaños!/Three Centuries to Remember* that Richard McCord and I authored. For me to have been their escort indeed was a distinct honor as well as a marvelous way to celebrate Albuquerque's 300th anniversary.

Lifetime Achievement Award, Historical Society of New Mexico (HSNM), 2012

On April 1, 2012, I was pleasantly surprised to receive a letter from Nancy Owen Lewis, chair, HSNM Awards Committee. "Congratulations! You have just been named the recipient of the Lifetime

Achievement Award by the Historical Society of New Mexico in recognition of your stellar contributions—as an educator, community activist, and author—to New Mexico history." The award was presented to me on May 5, 2012, at the Governor's Mansion in Santa Fe. To be honored by a stellar organization such as the Historical Society of New Mexico founded in 1859 whose members represent a diversity of interests within the annals of New Mexico history was extremely gratifying.

When the Stars Trembled in Río Puerco, 2014

This is an original play adapted from oral histories that I compiled from former Hispanic old-timers of my Río Puerco Valley. Ranching families live out scenes of land, loss, and community in four now ghost towns southwest of Cuba, New Mexico: a boy flees raiding parties, influenza decimates a family; a *viejita* recounts somber and funny rituals with saints/santos; another sings ballads about tragedies; together they recreate losing livelihoods and cattle to land regulations and narrate ghost stories about *brujerías*, witches and strange sights. As the characters say, "aunque nosotros olvidemos, el pasado recuerda" (Even if we forget, the past remembers). Written and directed by Shebana Coelho, the play features Rudy "Froggy' Fernández, Anna María Gonzales, Amador Gonzales, María Cristina López, Argos MacCallum, Oscar Rodríguez, and JoJo Sena de Tarnoff. The play was coproduced by Teatro Paraguas and Recuerdos Vivos New Mexico.

Hoe, Heaven, and Hell: My Boyhood in Rural New Mexico, *Multiple Awards,* 2015

Of the more than thirty books that bear my name, there are those devoted to oral history and folklore. But my short stories, both for adults and young adults, including my children's books and poetry (see Books Authored for a complete list) propel the reader back to my childhood.

One publication that stands out among my books is *Hoe, Heaven, and Hell: My Boyhood in Rural New Mexico.* The reason is quite simple and straightforward. My memoir not only pays homage to my beloved parents, but it also rekindles my early years in the Río Puerco Valley. Those days of yore laden with a potpourri of cultural trappings, be they celebrating the local fiestas in my village of Ojo del Padre (aka Guadalupe) or helping one's parents till the land to put food on the table, are gone forever.

Hoe, Heaven, and Hell: My Boyhood in Rural New Mexico, *International Latino Book Award,* 2016

In 2016 *Hoe, Heaven, and Hell* was awarded first place by the International Latino Book Awards for best autobiography. The New Mexico–Arizona Book Awards selected my memoir Best Biography—New Mexico Subject, and Best Book on New Mexico. The Historical Society of New Mexico accorded it the prestigious Fabiola Cabeza de Baca Award for an outstanding publication related to domestic life in New Mexico. The forgoing awards attest to the breadth and scope of remembrances contained in *Hoe, Heaven, and Hell.* That is what separates my biography from my other endearing books.

Documentary, Nasario Remembers the Río Puerco, 2017

Nasario Remembers the Río Puerco is a documentary produced/ directed by renowned filmmaker Shebana Coelho about landscape and memory, set in the ghost towns of New Mexico's Río Puerco Valley and features yours truly. The film combines footage of me and my stories amid ruins and mesas with archival photos and lyric scenes that evoke the storytelling spirits of my beloved valley. Together, these elements create a deeply felt cinematic encounter between teller and tale, what is gone and what is left of memory and coming home to the story that only the narrator can tell. Director-producer: Shebana Coelho. Cinematographer: Kelvin DuVal. Editor: Shelene Bridge.

John Nichols, author of *The Milagro Beanfield War* and *My Heart Belongs to Nature*, lauded the film: "A wonderful documentary . . . very moving. Just exquisite and very powerful. It's right up there with the best I've ever seen."

ALSO BY NASARIO GARCÍA

Books Authored and/or Coedited

García, Nasario. *Lágrimas: Poems of Joy and Sorrow*. Pittsburgh: Judith Literary Press, 2020.

———. *Grandma Lale's Magical Adobe Oven / El horno mágico de Abuelita Lale*. Albuquerque: Río Grande Books, 2019.

———. *No More Bingo, Comadre! Stories*. Albuquerque: University of New Mexico Press, 2018.

———. *Grandpa Lolo's Matanza: A New Mexico Tradition*. Albuquerque: Río Grande Books, 2016.

———. *Hoe, Heaven, and Hell: My Boyhood in Rural New Mexico*. Albuquerque: University of New Mexico Press, 2015.

———. *Grandma Lale's Tamales: A Christmas Story/Los tamales de Abuelita Lale: Un cuento navideño*. Albuquerque: Río Grande Books, 2014.

———. *Grandpa Lolo and Trampa: A Story of Surprise and Mystery / Abuelito Lolo y Trampa: Un cuento de sorpresa y misterio*. Albuquerque: Río Grande Books, 2014.

———. *The Talking Lizard: New Mexico's Magic and Mystery*. Albuquerque: Río Grande Books, 2014.

———. *Bernalillo: Yesterday's Sunshine—Today's Shadows*. Albuquerque: Río Grande Books, 2014.

————. *Grandma's Santo on Its Head: Stories of Days Gone By in Hispanic Villages of New Mexico / El santo patas arriba de mi abuelita: Cuentos de días gloriosos en pueblitos hispanos de Nuevo México.* Albuquerque: University of New Mexico Press, 2013.

————. *Grandpa Lolo's Navajo Saddle Blanket / La tilma de abuelito Lolo.* Albuquerque: University of New Mexico Press, 2012.

————. *An Indelible Imprint: A Multi-Talented Personality.* Albuquerque: Río Grande Books, 2011.

————. *Bolitas de oro: Poems of My Marble-Playing Days.* Albuquerque: University of New Mexico Press, 2010.

————. *Fe y tragedias: Faith and Tragedies in Hispanic Villages of New Mexico.* Albuquerque: Río Grande Books, 2010.

————. *Rattling Chains and Other Stories for Children / Ruido de cadenas y otros cuentos para niños.* Houston: Arte Público Press, 2009.

————. *The Naked Rainbow and Other Stories / El arco iris y otros cuentos.* Albuquerque: University of New Mexico Press, 2009.

————. *Brujerías: Stories of Witchcraft and the Supernatural in the American Southwest and Beyond.* Lubbock: Texas Tech University Press, 2007.

————. *Old Las Vegas: Hispanic Memories from the New Mexico Meadowlands.* Lubbock: Texas Tech University Press, 2005.

————, and Richard McCord. *Albuquerque ¡Feliz Cumpleaños!: Three Centuries to Remember.* Santa Fe, NM: La Herencia Publication, 2005.

————. *Chistes: Hispanic Humor of Northern New Mexico and Southern Colorado.* Santa Fe: Museum of New Mexico Press, 2004.

————. *Tiempos lejanos: Poetic Images from the Past.* Albuquerque: University of New Mexico Press, 2004.

————. *Comadres: Hispanic Women of the Río Puerco Valley*. Santa Fe: Western Edge Press, 2001.

————. *Pláticas: Conversations with Hispano Writers of New Mexico*. Lubbock: Texas Tech University Press, 2000.

————, ed. *Cantares: Canticles and Poems of Youth*, by Fray Angélico Chávez. Houston: Arte Público Press, 2000.

————. *Brujas, bultos, y brasas / Tales of Witchcraft and the Supernatural in the Pecos Valley*. Santa Fe: Western Edge Press, 1999.

————, and José B. Fernández, eds. *¿Cómo andas?, Curso intermedio de comunicación*. Upper Saddle River, NJ: Prentice Hall, 1998.

————. *Comadres: Hispanic Women of the Río Puerco Valley*. Albuquerque: University of New Mexico Press, 1997.

————. *Más antes: Hispanic Folklore of the Río Puerco Valley*. Santa Fe: Museum of New Mexico Press, 1997.

————. *Tata: A Voice from the Río Puerco*. Albuquerque: University of New Mexico Press (in cooperation with the Historical Society of New Mexico), 1994.

————. *Abuelitos: Stories of the Río Puerco Valley*. Albuquerque: University of New Mexico Press (in cooperation with the Historical Society of New Mexico), 1992.

————. *Recuerdos de los viejitos: Tales of the Río Puerco*. Albuquerque: University of New Mexico Press (in cooperation with the Historical Society of New Mexico), 1987.

————, and José B. Fernández, eds. *¿Qué hay de Nuevo?* Lexington, MA: D.C. Heath and Co., 1985.

————, and José B. Fernández, eds. *Nuevos horizontes*. Lexington, MA: D.C. Heath and Co., 1982.

————, and Larry Trujillo. *Festival folklórico mexicano*. Pueblo, CO: Sir Speedy Printers, 1976.

Books Translated

————. *I Dig This Book! / Me encanta este libro*, by Barbe Awalt. Albuquerque: Río Grande Books, 2018.

————. *Don't Touch this Book / No toques este libro*, by Barbe Awalt. Albuquerque: Río Grande Books, 2017.

————. *The Adventures of BernCo Bernie / Las aventuras de BernCo Bernie*, by Jill D. Lane. Albuquerque: Río Grande Books, 2015.

————. *How Chile Came to New Mexico / Cómo llegó el chile a Nuevo México*, by Rudolfo Anaya. Albuquerque: Río Grande Books, 2014.

————. *How Hollyhocks Came to New Mexico / Cómo llegaron las varas de San José a Nuevo México*, by Rudolfo Anaya. Albuquerque: Río Grande Books, 2012.

————. *West of Babylon / Al oeste de Babilonia*, by Eduardo Garrigues. Albuquerque: University of New Mexico Press, 2002.

————. *La tierra de las adivinanzas / The Land of Riddles*, by César Villarreal Elizondo. Houston: Arte Público Press, 2002.

BOOK AWARDS AND HONORS

Book Awards

2021

Lágrimas: Poems of Joy and Sorrow. Pittsburgh: Judith Literary Press, 2020.

> —First-Place Winner, Bilingual Poetry, New Mexico, New Mexico–
> Arizona Book Awards
> —Honorable Mention, International Latino Book Awards

2019

No More Bingo, Comadre! Stories. Albuquerque: University of New
Mexico Press, 2018.

> —First-Place Winner, Fiction New Mexico, New Mexico–Arizona
> Book Awards

*Grandma Lale's Magical Adobe Oven: El horno mágico de Abuelita
Lale*. Albuquerque: Río Grande Books, 2019.

—Winner, Pablita Velarde Award, Historical Society of New Mexico

—First-Place Winner, Children's Books, Fiction, New Mexico Press Women

—Second-Place Winner, Children's Book, National Federation of Press Women

—Winner, Cover Design-Fiction, New Mexico–Arizona Book Awards

—Finalist, Children's Picture Bilingual, New Mexico–Arizona Book Awards

2017

Grandpa Lolo's Matanza: A New Mexico Tradition. Albuquerque: Río Grande Books, 2016.

—First-Place Winner, Children's Books—Non-Fiction, National Federation of Press Women

—Winner, Children's Bilingual Book, New Mexico–Arizona Book Awards

—Second-Place Winner, Best Latino Focused Children's Picture Book—Bilingual, the International Latino Book Awards

—Honorable Mention, Best Use of Illustrations Inside the Book, the International Latino Book Awards

—Finalist, Young Reader, New Mexico–Arizona Book Awards

—Finalist, Multicultural Subject, New Mexico–Arizona Book Awards

—Finalist, Children's Picture Book, New Mexico–Arizona Book Awards

2016

Hoe, Heaven, and Hell: My Boyhood in Rural New Mexico.
Albuquerque: University of New Mexico Press, 2015.

—First-Place Winner, Best Autobiography—English, the International Latino Book Awards

—Winner, Best Book on New Mexico, New Mexico–Arizona Book Awards

—Winner, Biography—New Mexico Subject, New Mexico–Arizona Book Awards

—Winner, Fabiola Cabeza de Baca Award for an Outstanding Publication or Exhibit Related to Domestic Life in New Mexico, the Historical Society of New Mexico

Grandma Lale's Tamales: A Christmas Story. Albuquerque: Río Grande Books, 2014.

—Second-Place Winner, Best Latino Focused Children's Picture Book—Bilingual, the International Latino Book Awards

—Second-Place Winner, Best Latino Focused Book Design, the International Latino Book Awards

—Honorable Mention, Best Cover Design, the International Latino Book Awards

—Honorable Mention, Best Use of Illustrations Inside the Book, the International Latino Book Awards

2015

Bernalillo: Yesterday's Sunshine/Today's Shadows. Albuquerque: Río Grande Books, 2014.

—First-Place Winner, Best History Book—Spanish or Bilingual, the International Latino Book Awards

—First-Place Winner, Oral Short Stories, New Mexico Press Women

The Talking Lizard: New Mexico's Magic & Mystery. Albuquerque: Río Grande Books, 2014

—Winner, Young Readers. New Mexico–Arizona Book Awards

—Honorable Mention, Children's Book-Fiction (English and Spanish), New Mexico Press Women

Grandma Lale's Tamales: A Christmas Story. Albuquerque: Río Grande Books, 2014

—Winner, Pablita Velarde Award for Outstanding Publication or Significant Contribution to New Mexico or Southwest Borderlands History (Children's Story in English and Spanish), Historical Society of New Mexico

—Winner, Children's Picture and Activity Bilingual, New Mexico–Arizona Book Awards

—Second-Place Winner, Children's Book—Fiction (English and Spanish), New Mexico Press Women

Grandpa Lolo and Trampa: A Story of Surprise and Mystery. Albuquerque: Río Grande Books, 2014.

—Third-Place Winner, Children's Book—Fiction (English and Spanish), New Mexico Press Women

2014

Grandpa Lolo and Trampa: A Story of Surprise and Mystery.
Albuquerque: Río Grande Books, 2014.

—Winner, Young Readers' Book (to Grade 3), New Mexico–Arizona
Book Awards

Bernalillo: Yesterday's Sunshine/Today's Shadows. Albuquerque: Río
Grande Books, 2014.

—Winner, Best New Mexico, New Mexico–Arizona Book Awards

Grandma's Santo on Its Head: El Santo patas arriba de mi abuelita.
Albuquerque: University of New Mexico Press, 2013.

—Finalist, New Mexico–Arizona Book Awards

2013

Grandma's Santo on Its Head: El Santo patas arriba de mi abuelita.
Albuquerque: University of New Mexico Press, 2013.

—Western Heritage Award for Outstanding Juvenile Book, National
Cowboy and Western Heritage Museum, Oklahoma City

Grandpa Lolo's Navajo Saddle Blanket/La tilma de Abuelito Lolo.
Albuquerque: University of New Mexico Press, 2012.

—Winner, Southwest Book Award, the Border Regional Library
Association, El Paso, Texas
—Second-Place Winner, Best Children's Picture Book—English,
the International Book Awards

—Selection by New Mexico State Library Staff to Represent New Mexico in the Pavilion of the States at the National Book Festival (Sponsored by the Library of Congress) in Washington, DC, September 21–22 on the National Mall

2012

An Indelible Imprint: Rubén Cóbos, A Multi-Talented Personality. Albuquerque: Río Grande Books, 2011.

—Finalist, New Mexico–Arizona Book Awards

2010

Rattling chains and Other Stories/Ruido de cadenas y otros cuentos. Houston: Arte Público Press, 2009.

—Finalist, New Mexico–Arizona Book Awards

Fe y tragedias: Faith and Tragedies. Albuquerque: Río Grande Books, 2010.

—Finalist, New Mexico–Arizona Book Awards

2009

The Naked Rainbow and Other Stories: El arco iris y otros cuentos. Albuquerque: University of New Mexico Press, 2009.

—Southwest Book of the Year, Pima County Public Library, Tucson, Arizona

2008

Brujerías: Stories of Witchcraft and the Supernatural in the American Southwest and Beyond. Lubbock: Texas Tech University Press, 2007.

—Finalist, New Mexico–Arizona Book Awards

2007

Brujerías: Stories of Witchcraft and the Supernatural in the American Southwest and Beyond. Lubbock: Texas Tech University Press, 2007.

—Southwest Book of the Year, Pima County Public Library, Tucson, Arizona

2006

Old Las Vegas: Hispanic Memories from the New Mexico Meadowlands. Albuquerque: Río Grande Books, 2005.

—Southwest Book Award, Border Regional Library Association, El Paso, Texas

Honors

2017: "Diploma en consideración a los conocimientos lingüísticos, méritos literarias y demás ejecutorias" (Diploma in consideration of linguistic knowledge, literary merits, and other accomplishments related to the Spanish language). Signed, New York City, August 27, 2017, by the director and secretary of the Academia

Nacional de la Lengua Española.

2012: Life-Time Achievement Award, Historical Society of New Mexico.

2010: Recognized as Friend of New Mexico Books, New Mexico–Arizona Book Awards Banquet, Albuquerque, New Mexico.

2006: Excellence in Historical Programming, *Albuquerque Revisited: Three Centuries to Remember, 1706–2006*, Albuquerque Historical Society.

1999–2000: Zía Award, Distinguished Alumnus, University of New Mexico.

1991–1992: Phi Eta Sigma Freshman Honor Society, Recognition of Excellence in Teaching, New Mexico Highlands University.

1988–1989: New Mexico Eminent Scholar, Commission on Higher Education.

1983–1984: Scholarship Award, Colorado Congress of Foreign Language Teachers.

1982–1983: Recipient, Outstanding Faculty Owl Award, University of Southern Colorado.

1981–1982: Recipient, Outstanding Faculty Owl Award, University of Southern Colorado.

1977–1978: Recipient, Outstanding Faculty Owl Award, University of Southern Colorado.

1976–1977: Nominee, Educator of the Year Award, Excellence in Teaching Performance, University of Southern Colorado Students.